A Deed Without a Name

Unearthing the Legacy of Traditional Witchcraft

A Deed Without a Name

Unearthing the Legacy of Traditional Witchcraft

Lee Morgan

MOON

BOOKS

Winchester, UK
Washington, USA

First published by Moon Books, 2013
Moon Books is an imprint of John Hunt Publishing Ltd., Laurel House, Station Approach,
Alresford, Hants, SO24 9JH, UK
office1@jhpbooks.net
www.johnhuntpublishing.com
www.moon-books.net

For distributor details and how to order please visit the 'Ordering' section on our website.

Text copyright: Lee Morgan 2012

ISBN: 978 1 78099 549 6

A CIP catalogue record for this book is available from the British Library.

Design: Stuart Davies

Printed and bound by CPI Group (UK) Ltd, Croydon, CR0 4YY

We operate a distinctive and ethical publishing philosophy in all
areas of our business, from our global network of authors to
production and worldwide distribution.

CONTENTS

Macbeth   -*How now, you secret, black, and midnight Hags?*
What is't you do?
All - A deed without a name.

-William Shakespeare: *Macbeth*

Dedication

For my fetch-mate, Magistellus R-, without you I am both Artless and wordless. You gave me your fire, and I only had my heart to give you in return. In everything I write or do I strive to be worthy of your gift.

Acknowledgments

I'd like to thank my partner Brett Morgan, first and foremost, for both his support and the wonderful artwork he has contributed to this book. Without his encouragement I would probably have become discouraged with the task of bringing this work into being. I'd also like to thank the wonderful Rebecca Flynn for her scrupulous red pen and attention to detail. The idea behind this book would probably not have come to be in the first place if not for the witches of the Anderean Coven, of which I am privileged to be a part; so thank you all. And to all of my wider witchcraft network who contributed testimonials, thank you for sharing your experiences with me, and trusting me to present them here.

A Deed Without a Name

Darkness adopted illumination in order to make itself visible.
-Robert Fludd

We all know stories about witchcraft; some of us even think we know the 'truth' about it. What we often forget is that whilst there is an ancient and eternal 'deed without a name' that lies behind the word, the word itself is little more than a site where numerous tales cluster. Those who choose the path, or are chosen for the path, of witchcraft usually have a gut-level sense of what the word means. They are drawn inexorably to a collection of images, a vague narrative which has to do with night-flights in spirit form, the crossing of hedges and boundaries, boiling cauldrons and wild dances in wild places where the dead appear, and where animal transformation and acts of sorcery occur.

The scholarly among us may ask questions about how much

of the image of the witch was created by the interrogator? Others are happy to accept the received knowledge as it stands. Those who consult scholarship too often err on the side of the arm-chair occultist, reading tomes upon tomes of books and journal articles, practicing 'witchcraft in the head' without finding a way to bridge the gap between scholarship and practice. Others do not keep track of the sizeable advances in modern witchcraft scholarship and thus miss out on much enlightening material. This book attempts to bridge the gap between these extremes.

It aims to shine the light of reason into the darkness of the wild and waste places outside the hedge. But unlike those who usually carry the lantern of scholarship I am an experienced practical occultist and witch. I do not go there to look into the shadows as someone to whom darkness is foreign and who wishes to tame it with my intellect through ordering and categorising. I know the darkness as a Mother, and the darkness Herself knows me as one of Her own. I take this light of reason with me to illuminate for others something that I myself am familiar with, and because this light, or 'fire', is also part of my inheritance as a human being.

Whilst I have become comfortable in those gloaming spaces I know that we moderns are not able to fully return to primal darkness on its own terms. As Fate has it, we are bearers of the flame of civilisation and find ourselves a long way from the mindset of the witches of old, who met spirits at styles and crossroads with seeming ease. And yet what I discover through kindling up my flame and taking it into unexpected places, is that we are also never far from those shadows; they nestle in the base of our skulls and in our guts, as well as in the woodland outside the hedge, part of our inheritance also. So this work is dedicated to a pursuit of the half forgotten legacy of witchcraft and the *myth* of witchcraft, one that pays homage both to the lantern of the seeking mind and the rich, fecund darkness from which that mind draws its life. In seeking the 'legacy' of an essentially nameless act I will be forced to tell stories and repeat stories, as tales, because shared narratives are what we are really talking about when we talk about 'traditions'.

For many decades witchcraft trial records were seen as largely fictional narratives that therefore had little value in understanding the real 'truth' behind these confessions. They were viewed in terms of the power of the inquisitor over the victim and seldom in the context of the wider belief system of European folklore. Scholars were too afraid of being accused of 'Murrayism'; that is the belief, along with the early scholar Margaret Murray (so influential upon Wicca) that the trial records represent proof of a 'witch cult' replete with covens of thirteen run by literal priests in devil's costumes.

Whilst Murray's thesis has been largely discredited other scholars have reopened this field as a viable area of study. Carlos Ginzburg began the important work of showing the witches' 'flight' as a shamanic-style leaving of the body by a 'Double', rather than a literal and therefore impossible story. Since then we have been inclined to look at the multiple witchcraft narratives differently. Many scholars have begun to look at them in terms of 'things believed to be true' by people, regardless of their truth value as 'literal facts' and others have gone further and made comparisons with shamanism in other nations. It is my aim to make the practical implications of this witchcraft scholarship available through the lens of my own occult experience, namely in Traditional Witchcraft.

This project, and the book it became, is the result of a rather fey coincidence. Over the years as I collected the experiences of myself and my contemporaries I often discovered, after the fact, that this experiential material could now be supported or even better explained by scholarly material on the topic. On its own a vision, a swirling form out of the body of the darkness, that wells into the mind of a single person may be seen as an anomaly. But when those forms begin to create patterns and repetitions the attention of the light of reason is warranted. I decided that it was high time for someone to attempt a synthesis between this wealth of scholarly information and this continuingly growing practical knowledge-base, one that would have value for the practical student of non-wiccan, post-Christian, European witchcraft.

The implications of the works of such scholars as Carlos Ginzburg[1], Eva Pocs[2], Claude Lecouteux[3] and most notably and recently, Emma Wilby, all provided me with elements of the material here. Juxtaposed both with my practical experience in current witchcraft and a wealth of folkloric material I am able to put this scholarly progress in a context that is useful for those who wish to practice rather than simply read about witchcraft. But I have done so in a way that goes beyond the typical 'recipe book of spells' model, and tries to cut deeper into the marrow of what this legacy really is and means.

Emma Wilby's work *'The Visions of Isobel Gowdie: Magic, Witchcraft and Dark Shamanism in Seventeenth Century Scotland'*[4] in particular poses large and weighty questions about the practice of Witchcraft, for those who are engaged in it. Her comparative work between witches like Isobel Gowdie and the 'dark shamans' of the Amazon Basin is extremely compelling and forces us to ask perhaps the most important questions of all about 'witchcraft.' What is a witch? And what deeper function did witches originally fulfil, not just for their community but also for the unseen world of the spirit?

Wilby shows how Isobel and her coven acted essentially as 'Fates' that often dealt malignant blows upon mankind, that when Isobel is called 'witch' it means something entirely different to when the 'faerie witch' Bessie Dunlop is named 'witch'. Unlike Isobel, Bessie's contact with the world of faerie led her to offer cures and healing to sick children, adults and animals. This being said, the sum of the evidence suggests that these services offered by some witches were only the tip of the ice burg in terms of the deeper *meaning* of witchcraft at a cosmological level.

One might be tempted to simply correct this sloppy use of terminology by giving Isobel the appellation 'black witch' and Bessie: 'white witch.' But the matter is not so simple. A quick glance at the work of Carlos Ginzburg on the *benandanti* and his comparative work on Werewolves (a topic also covered in detail by Eva Pocs) shows us that the Otherworldly experiences placed under the heading of 'witchcraft' were far more diverse than can be simply ordered into 'black' and 'white' versions of the same phenomena. Now of course, much of this diversity is drawn from continental sources, but I believe there is evidence enough to suggest that this diversity would have once been more general in Britain as well as the continent. The Sicilian 'faerie trials' as they were called, where dozens of women and a few men were accused of being 'faerie-magicians', consorting with the King and Queen of faerie and deriving powers to heal from there, are strikingly similar to the 'faerie-doctors' of Ireland and to Bessie Dunlop of Scotland. Isobel Gowdie makes us think more of the *'malandanti'*, with her cursing and blighting behaviour, than the *benandanti* (good walkers) who fought against them for the preservation of the crops! It is suggested here that it is both useful to continue calling ourselves 'witches' and at the same time that we will discover there to be many kinds of 'witches'.

The 'deed without a name', mankind's innate ability to have contact with another world and participate, often ecstatically, in its doings, (something more pronounced in some than others), came to find a name in Europe under the word 'witchcraft.' It would be easy for the scholarly among us to dislike the term or even reject it. Indeed, in a sense, by spreading a blanket over all spiritual experiences that were Other and calling them 'witchcraft' the witch-hunter did us a great disservice and lost or obscured a lot of rich and divergent forms of sorcery and ecstatic experience. But in another sense, a sense of turning the 'devil of perversity' upon itself, it also opens up the possibility of a brotherhood of the Other. And it is in this spirit that I approach the term.

Through a careful mix of scholarship and experience there is no reason we cannot also claim back some of the variety behind the term today, and enjoy both the unity and the diversity. For it is unlikely that these many powers that erupted into the psyche of Europe in the past have utterly ceased to do so, or ceased to manifest in diverse forms because we have all but ceased to recognise them. And through reawakening this understanding I believe that as an Art we can move closer to less of a 'one size fits all' approach to the unseen. Once we did not all ride broomsticks, but some of us rode on ragwort, stangs or pitchforks, fennel, sorghum, goats, wolves, cats or required no stead because we simply transformed into beasts ourselves. And yet, at the same time, we needn't deny the broomstick as a symbol that has come to unite us. For really the symbolism of the broom goes a little deeper than just habit or stereotype.

It is noted that witches were inclined to fly on brooms, stangs, pitchforks, distaffs and even ladles which can initially seem a little strange. But when we realise that in Hungary, for instance, when the drum became something that could no longer be owned for fear of being caught using it to go into a trance state, it gradually became replaced by the sieve, a common household object that could be pressed into the service of the unseen.[4] These common household objects are a testimony to how the world outside the hedge continually interpenetrates with everything inside it, everything mundane and seemingly normal and unthreatening remains subtly imbued with its Other. In a world where 'witchcraft', a practice always partially hidden, became something that had to hide, it *was able to hide,* behind every teapot, ladle, broom and kettle on the stovetop.

Who is Called and Who is Calling?

...Queen of our inner country, that landscape which is usually called the Soul. She knows its highways and turnings, its valleys and its peaks. Her language is poetry and where she walks dreams spring up behind her like small white flowers.
-Edward Whitmont

There is a key question when it comes to witchcraft, and yet it is too often skipped right over. We talk about being here, or walking down the 'crooked path' because of a call, and too often neglect to ask 'who is calling'? And where does this 'crooked path' lead?

The very term 'the crooked path' suggests at first glance that the path of witchcraft is the opposite path to that of Christianity. The term is in fact related to the tradition of 'sacred walking', of walking for meditative purposes by early Celtic Christians on pilgrimage. These tracks were laid out to connect sites of holy significance and being on the 'straight and narrow path' symbolised the meditative walkers adherence to God.[6] As an old Gaelic maxim tells us, 'He who will not take advice will take the crooked track.'

But like with many seemingly 'Christian reversals' that have found their way into the witchcraft legacy there is more to this notion of the 'crooked path' than simply doing the opposite to the church. Like Hermes' Caduceus the 'straight tracks' around Britain (and other locations) and the human spine itself, the straight path is always coiled around by twin serpent lines. In the case of these twining 'serpent lines' in the land numerous ancient pagan holy sites emerge along them. It seems that our ancestors set out these holy sites both to recognise the straight track down the middle and the crooked one that twined around it. Like the migratory path of geese, something often associated with the host of the dead in flight along the 'ghost tracks'; these straight tracks are best appreciated from the air. The 'crooked' snaking paths around them however are very much the path of the walker, they penetrate the land with many a holy well and standing stone.

So we might say that in reviling the serpent, in reviling this crooked and snaking path, it was walking the path of the earth and its interior that the Christian saints were rejecting. It also implies that if we agree to walk this path we accept the 'hooks and crooks' of the road that may obscure what lies ahead and agree to follow the irregularities of the earth's path and be guided by our intuition. We could even say that in the context of this book, itself an exercise in meditative walking, that the scholarly component of witchcraft lore is the 'straight track' and the path of experiential gnosis via occult practice is the 'crooked road' that winds and snakes around it.

If this is the path that someone walks in becoming a witch then how does someone know they have been called to become a witch, and what makes someone a witch? It seems that from the available records there were two broad scenarios that occurred in the past. The first scenario is that the individual is in some sense 'born that way'. Without any human intervention they are approached by spirits or even the 'Devil' himself and informed of their vocation or gifted with powers. This notion of being a 'born witch' or a 'blood witch' has found its way into the revival movement at many levels and is reviled in some quarters. The second scenario is that the individual was brought into their vocation by another human being. They may share a toast from a tankard with a werewolf, a witch may invite them to a sabbat and they agree three times that they will come, or they may have one hand placed over their head and one under their foot by a faerie-seer and thus made able to see as they could see. We can tell from this second method that a type of 'spiritual contagion' was both believed in and consciously practiced.

The way that the future witch is called is determined by *what they are called on to do*. I believe that this element of function and service, both to this world and the Otherworld, is something that we have all but forgotten in modern witchcraft in favour of a path primarily about self-discovery. Whilst self-discovery and ones own spiritual evolution is inarguably an important occult aim, it appears that there was more to the bigger picture of witchcraft in the past.

The future *benandanti*, for instance, might experience his first ride with his fellows and meet with other men he knows in his human life whilst doing so. He may then receive a mixture of human and Otherworldly instruction. He is then expected to perform a very clear spiritual function that he believed had immediate and measurable results for his community around him. It is also quite clear from the beginning, given what we have said about Isobel Gowdie and the *malandanti* that not all 'witches' are being called to work for the same forces. But fortunately for us we are able to apply an understanding of Fate, and through this we can see that whatever else divided these various types of ecstatic sorcerers they all, fundamentally, work for Fate or Grandmother

Weaver. Some are involved in managing the 'out breath' of the land and others in Her 'in breath'. And they do so as necessary representations of the giving and taking forces of life and death.

Whatever the form of 'call' that a witch received one can only imagine it must have been strong and compelling. People chose to answer these calls under threat of excommunication, banishment, torture and death. I believe this to be the yardstick, against which modern interest in witchcraft should be measured, something that gives us respect for the potency of the powers we intend to engage with. To put it simply: *these people experienced the truth of these phenomena so strongly they were willing to risk their lives to engage with them.* Or perhaps even more simply, they literally had no choice...

Today we do not usually put ourselves at risk of such things by practicing our Art. But risks have not entirely disappeared. So before undertaking to disturb the powers of the wild and waste spaces beyond the hedge, it is probably worth considering if you have any other choice. Have entities beyond this world already reached out for you? Or did another person come into your life and show you something that you just can't turn your back on now you've seen it? If either of these things apply to you there will doubtlessly be much of value to you in this book. If they don't then it may just be the case that this book was the fateful trigger you were destined to find.

Here are a few examples of testimonials from witches from the past about their 'call'. It is quite clear that they are not all called by the same entity or entities, and yet there are commonalities running throughout:

She told them that when she was a child of eight, she had flown through the air with a group of women on goats to a vast field on the mainland of the Kingdom of Naples called Benevento, where a red-haired teenage boy and a beautiful woman sat on a throne.

According to her confession, they were called the King and the Queen. She said that the leader of the women who took her there, who was called the Ensign, told her that if she fell to her knees in front of the King and Queen of the elves and gave them allegiance, they would give her riches, beauty and handsome men, with whom she could have sex, and that she was not to worship God or the holy Virgin.

-'Fairy-magician', witch of Sicily

As I was goeing betuix the townes of Drumdewin and the Headis, I met with The Devil, and ther covenanted,in a maner, with him.

-Isobel Gowdie, witch of Scotland

I went on those three days because others told me to... the first one to tell me to go was Giambattista Tamburlino... he informed me that he and I were benandanti, and that I had to go with him. And when I replied that I would not go, he said, 'When you have to come, you will come.' And to this I declared, 'You will not be able to make me,' and he, in turn, insisted 'You will have to come anyway, one goes as though in a smoky haze, we do not go physically,' and said that we had to go and fight for the faith, even though I kept saying that I didn't want to go.

-Menichino, *Benandanti*[7] of Fruili

I will do it as it was done to me: I will drink someone's health and blow three times into the jug, saying: 'may what happens to me happen to you.' If the other person takes the jug, I won't be a werewolf anymore.

-Thiess, Werewolf of Livonia

I have indeed observed that mazzerisme runs in certain families: the mazzeru I met had originally been 'called' by an uncle, a mazzera confided to me that she had initiated her daughter.

-*Mazzera* of Corsica

This Bastiano used to come with me to a pasture where his master's animals grazed; he became friendly, and I asked him in the pasture if he wanted to come with me and the witches to dance; he said yes, he would come. I repeated this a second time when we were at the pasture; he told me that he would come and then I said to him, 'I shall come to call you at night, don't be afraid, we shall go together.' And so I did: the following Thursday I mounted my goat and went to find Bastiano who was in bed, I called him by his name and said to him: 'Bastiano, do you want to come with me to the dance of the witches?' And he replied, 'Yes, I do." I had another goat with me, and Bastiano mounted it, and together we rode off to the dance of the witches in Santa Catarina's Field.

    -Daniel Soppe, Italian Witch

While she was taking her cow out to a field, she came across an elderly man with a grey beard wearing a grey coat. He wore a black bonnet on his head, and carried a white wand in his hand. He said that he was the spirit of Thomas Reid, a former Baron Officer to John Blair of Dalry, who had been killed at the battle of Pinkie in 1547. At that time Bessie was stressed with worry, her child, husband and cow were ill, and it seemed they might die. The old man comforted her and predicted that her cow and child would die, but her husband would make a full recovery. He then walked off towards the yard of Moncastle, and disappeared down a hole in a dyke that was much too small to let any mortal man pass by it. This was to be her first meeting with the man who would act as her familiar.

    -Bessie Dunlop, 'faerie witch' of Scotland

By way of comparison to the older testimonies below are some anonymous quotes taken from modern witches whose personal veracity I am able to vouch for. Whilst I have occult ties with all informants not all of them know the others nor did any contributor know the contents of the book they were contributing to. I have included them to show the way in which diversity has naturally emerged even today among those called to witchcraft, our Brotherhood of the Other. I have not chosen to give any kind of label to any of them other than 'witch', as I'd prefer to let the material speak for itself.

I first saw my familiar as a young child. This was the only time anything like this happened in my childhood. I got out of bed and went to the back window and opened the curtain. I don't know how I knew to get out of bed and go there. There on the back lawn was a tall man and a boy about my own age. I felt no shock at seeing them. I returned to my bed. In the morning I knew I got out of my bed and went there because the curtain was still moved. I didn't see anything again until I was about fourteen. One night I simply got out of my bed and believed I went in my body. I opened the front door and went out. There was the young boy I had seen but now he was grown to the same age or older than me. He was on a horse and he encouraged me to follow him. He took me to a spot in the road where a crossroads was that did not exist in real life. There was an old man there who showed me symbols. I was made to pick two of the objects he offered me. I was not taken like this again for many years, not until I had a kind of breakdown and that world opened up like that again. After it did I was taken away more often and the young man who I now know as a familiar, took me to meet the people he says are my 'faerie family.' He teaches me to heal and gives me things to write down. When I return I frequently crave and drink large quantities of milk.
    -Modern witch

My first call was during a dream when I was five. I lived on a farm and I dreamed once that there was a small shack in the field adjacent to my house, where one did not exist. There was a small old woman who invited me in and began to show me plants and announced that she was a 'witch'. It was the first time I remember hearing the word and the experience stuck with me thereafter. About the same time, I was having nightmares about people cutting me in my sleep, but no one believed me. We later found evidence that our house was built on a really old cemetery and no one moved the bodies.

-Modern witch

I was a few days old, and was sound asleep. It was late at night, and both my parents were alseep in the next room. When my mother woke suddenly, she found my Father sitting upright in bed, staring at the open door to their room. She sat up, but Dad didn't respond, he just stared blankly. She followed his gaze, and there in the open doorway stood a man. Mum always said she knew straight away who it was, and she felt knew she had to get up. When she did, apparently my Dad tried to prevent her, she told him it would be all right. The both got up out of bed and stood in front of this man, who turned and walked round the corner into my room. My parents followed and stood in my open doorway watching as this figure bent down and kissed me on the forehead.

As a little girl I often woke, half terrified, half desperate to call out 'Far Far?!" to see this man standing by my doorway. Whenever I woke he would slip outside, as if he was waiting quietly until I acknowledged him, as he did with my parents. Since I have consciously begun to practice the Craft and have spoken with him many times, he has taught me many things, he has been a great teacher. But I still wake sometimes to see him standing by the doorway. Only now I am not terrified, but grateful.

-Modern witch

I had been practicing the occult for years without any massive impact on my spiritual life. I was really at something of a crossroads in my life, and was questioning everything that I had been previously doing. Finally, at a loss, I 'gave up' if you like, and put it out there that I wasn't going to try anymore, but was ready for the universe to 'do it's worse'. Shortly after I made such a resolution I received a series of extremely vivid dreams. They were dreams of myself running from a pack of black dogs. Sometimes I would wake up before I was caught. Other times I was actually staked to the ground and could not run away. Sometimes there was only one dog. Other times there were many. They were all ridiculously large with sulphurous red eyes. And in the dream they would rip out my throat and gnaw on my insides. And then the dreams changed and the dogs would vomit molten lava back into the cavities in my body caused by my now consumed organs.

Once I dreamed a great black dog ripped open my guts and chewed its way up under my torso and I felt its teeth latch onto the base of my brain. The dreams were so physical. -And so vivid. I remember being quite agitated at the time. Of constantly seeing ghosts and weird visions at really inappropriate times. I would swerve the car to avoid hitting people that I saw out of the corner of my eye only to realise after a second they weren't physically there. I was anxious and moody, and constantly looked like I was angry when I wasn't. Then there was the nights where I had to go to bed. I simply passed out and began lucid dreaming. It started with an itching in my teeth. And as soon as I lay down I felt myself emerge, teeth first, out of my own mouth as a spectral black dog. And I would run and hunt. At first things would appear to me as white rabbits with devilish eyes. And I knew by consuming them they would be sent back from where they came for within me was a sulphurous pit which I had witnessed from the others in the pack. At other times the figure we hunted were people shaped and I assume they were souls or revenants not meant to be where we were hunting.

-Modern witch

As a young and only child I was often accompanied by my Familiar. Then known to me as my 'imaginary friend', we would meet high in branches and beneath hedgerows. He beckoned and I followed, leading me through childhood as my constant companion. As a teenager I lost him, forgot him, though in truth I sought him every-

where, in everyone. Filled with a nameless and desperate longing, searching with a fire in my belly for fulfilment, I found us both beneath the hawthorn, a decade later, and have come to know now both his ways and mine. My fetch-mate shows me visions and awakens my passions, he fills me with fire and asks for my fidelity. As a child I would hear voices, see ghosts and share premonitions of things to come, and learnt quickly to keep such things secret after being chastised, shamed and shunned by my elders. An 'odd' child, I was often to be found at the bottom of the garden; gathering flowers for both fairy folk and Familiar, performing elaborate and sombre burials for fallen feathered friends then exhuming said dead to fiddle with their bones, making ritualistic dances for the walnut tree and leaving offerings for the vegetable patch. My earliest memories of being in my body are of rocking, side to side whilst seated. And I still find said 'rocking' to be the quickest way to other places, to induce trance, to open my other eyes and to make things happen.

-Modern witch

The Witch as 'Shaman'

Flesh both inscribes and incorporates cultural memory and history... Knowing is corporeal. One mimes to understand. We copy the world to understand through our bodies.
-Paul Stoller

It could easily be said that one of the major differences between the modern revival referred to as 'Traditional Witchcraft' and the other modern revival known as 'Wicca', is that Traditional Witchcraft draws on 'folkloric material' and is largely 'shamanic' whereas Wicca is more of a fusion of Western Occult ceremonial and natural magic traditions. Whilst the term 'shamanic' is hotly debated both within scholarly and witchcraft circles it does at least seem clear that the term is cautiously embraced by the most influential scholars on the topic, the work of such people as Ginzburg and Wilby, texts that have greatly influenced the revival and self conception of 'Traditional Witchcraft' (especially

Ginzburg but I anticipate the same for Wilby's work as it becomes disseminated and assimilated into the occult group consciousness).

The exposition of the 'shamanic' dimension that Ginzburg worked so hard to establish in his books is what saves the study of the trial records from the excesses of 'Murrayism'. And the realisation that these testimonies were often to things encountered during spirit flight rather than in normative waking consciousness helps to make sense of the elements of the seeming impossible that occur in them. Emma Wilby took this work still further via a detailed comparison between the maleficium practiced during spirit flight by a witch like Isobel Gowdie and the 'dark shamans' of the Amazon Basin.

I believe that to properly navigate the 'deep myth' of witchcraft, and unearth the legacy of its occult wisdom we need to understand its shamanic substrata. But we need to understand the term 'shamanic' or perhaps even better 'ecstatic' in terms of a latent but universal potential within human nature, rather than strictly in sociological or anthropological terms. An 'ecstatic' is a type of mystic who leaves or transcends the flesh in powerful visions and has congress with another world. But a 'shaman' is one who uses this ability to perform a service for their community. We can see as we go along that many of these witches from the past fell into the latter category and that nearly all of them at least fell into the former.

Whilst the state of ecstasy is usually described as 'transcending the flesh' it is important to note that the witches' ecstatic vision grows out of the flesh as a plant does from soil. There may be visions of flying through the air, or going in through doors underground, but right from the beginning it will help us in our journey if we understand how rooted in biological experience vision is. Intensely sensual experiences (sensual as in 'of the senses) are involved in reaching trance for most people. Drumming, dance, sexual intercourse, imbibing helper plants and even being 'lifted' by spirits, all produce intense sensations and chemical releases in the body. Understanding these responses and how the bodily experience of our ancestors might have differed from our own can only help us in finding the keys to our own ecstasis. It will help us to remember the old maxim 'as above so below, as within so without', for it shows us a world where microcosm mirrors macrocosm.

Thus when we try to re-imagine a shamanic universe with an Upperworld above a Middleworld all around us and an Underworld below it is easier to get in touch with if we are aware that they also exist inside our bodies. Whilst the Underworld and Upperworld also exist outside of us, and reach beyond us we are each connected to them and reflect the structure of the universe. What all this means is that an ecstatic path is both a path of the body and of transcending the body, it is not a matter of either/or, but of both.

The Upperworld is reflected in our heads and the Underworld deep in out guts and pelvis, we each are made up of the substance of stars and of the dirt and water we drink daily and thus no part of the cosmos is foreign to us. We are part of the earth, our consciousness grows out of our flesh, and yet there is that within us that goes beyond it and joins the cosmos. It is to this mystery that I allude when I speak of 'shamanic' or 'ecstatic' witchcraft.

Marked as Other

I sometimes feel when I am wandering around in the marshes of the old knowledge, that the dam upstream is going to burst and the whole of humanity is going to be submerged by fifty thousand years of pre-history, swamping the neat subtopian conventions of the last thousand years.
    -Robert Cochrane

The concept of being 'marked' for witchcraft was in no way invented by the inquisitors. But as usual their understanding of the mark was reductive. In witch-hunting lore 'the mark' came to mean either the mark placed upon you by the 'Devil' when he drew your blood to sign your pact at your infernal baptism, or a sort of hidden 'teat' through which you suckled your imp (a smaller kind of familiar usually appearing in animal form.)

The first of these meanings has become a valid kind of witch-craft tradition. Even though it was once not the case that all 'witches' got their power in this way, taking a pact and being marked has become a gesture of solidarity and pride among our 'brotherhood of the Other'. Today it takes the form of an agreement between the witch and the Otherworldly powers they work with and sometimes with other human witches, to practice along certain lines and keep certain oaths. Pacts between human and Otherworldly agents and between witches when they form a coven have the power to bind groups of people of otherwise different natures together and establish common goals.

As valid as the 'mark on the left hand' (or shoulder for that matter) might be, it should not be seen as the sole meaning of the word 'marked.' If you search through the lore of the various types of ecstatic sorcerers who were named 'witches' and in many cases came to think of themselves as witches, you will see a great variety of 'marks'.

A *benandanti* was marked by being born with a caul and seems to have also been recognisable to their own kind in some other subtle way. *Taltos* (please see 'The Bestiary' under T for a full explanation) were born with a full set of teeth and craved dairy products. Being the seventh son of a seventh son could destine you to be a werewolf. Red hair was associated with strong tendencies toward witchcraft, lycanthropy or vampirism. Sixth fingers were strongly associated with witchcraft in the Tudor period to the extent that Anne Boleyn was accused of having one to justify the suspicion of witchcraft against her. In fact asymmetries of any kind, especially lameness in one foot, have been explored in detail in Ginzburg's *Ecstasies: Deciphering the Witches Sabbat.* Having one foot in some way impaired was associated with the Devil and his split foot and also with having 'one foot in the Otherworld.' One blind eye had the same meaning and is an attribute similar to Odin's missing eye, in that the other eye is always trained on the unseen.

Taken from a modern perspective it is easy to see that something 'backwards' or asymmetrical or simply strange, would easily function as a mark from the Otherness. And even today it is observable that many practicing witches experience some degree of Otherness, either physically, in relation to their sexuality or simply in their way of thinking. It is a worldwide phenomenon in many shamanic cultures that one can 'spot' the emergent shamanic temperament. Identifiable attributes range from quiet, strange thoughtful children who talk to a lot of 'imaginary friends' through to exceedingly precocious intelligence and abilities at an early age. In some cultures these children are traditionally sickly and fragile and come into their own only when the power comes upon them, some remain delicate for life. In other cultures they are extremely robust, more so than normal. The Hungarian *taltos* was on the 'robust' end of this extreme: He (and sometimes she) was naturally quarrelsome, loudly and energetically spoken, impatient to be on the move and a voracious eater.[8]

We have, in our own language a word for being 'marked' in the psychological sort of way. The word 'fey' before it became confounded with the word 'fay' and encountered much subsequent abuse, originally meant both 'visionary', 'touched' and possibly even 'fated to die.' The true shaman or witch does of course 'die' sooner than everyone else, one way or the other. So it is likely that this word was originally linked to the notion of the mark.

The Key That Fits No Lock

The Body of Flesh is the Vault of Ancestral Wisdom; it is the Silent Teacher of a Living Truth.
- Andrew Chumbley

One of the initial problems with calling the witchcraft testimonials and old witchcraft lore that comes down to us 'shamanic' or even 'ecstatic' is that witnesses were often unclear about whether they did a certain thing 'in their body' or in spirit. In fact, some actually swear that all of it occurred physically. So to better penetrate into this arcane territory we need to undertake a more thorough investigation into older ways of seeing the world.

When we look at the testimonials in the chapter above, one of the most obvious differences between the old and new material is that the modern witches mostly feel pretty clear about what happened 'while they were awake' and what happened in dreams, or whether they were 'in their body.' Some people might feel intimidated by the intensity of the experience that is indicated by this lack of clarity between states. It suggests such a compelling potency of direct Otherworldly experience that many of us moderns tend to wonder if we could ever see such things, ever be immersed in the knowledge of their total truth, and live them the way these witches and were-people did. Well, here I would like to draw on some of the observations of Lecouteux and Wilby in relation to 'the old way of seeing', and put them toward our practical occult goals.

In his book *The Return of the Dead: the transparent veil of the pagan mind* Lecouteux exposes us to older definitions of 'body' and 'soul' that are ultimately heathen in origin. He shows in detail how Christianity went about 'de-corporealising' the soul and making it into an immaterial thing. To our ancestors there was no such thing as an 'immaterial' thing. Everything had a kind of body; some of them were just denser and more easily perceived by humans than others.

Emma Wilby also touches on this when she speaks of the question posed by many witch-interrogators: 'did you do all this in your body or in spirit?' Although Christianity was long established in Scotland by this time, these ancient ideas seem to have lingered on up until at least the seventeenth century. Today we feel very clear about what is meant when someone says 'body' because we are in the habit of believing that we have only one. We also believe that whatever the 'soul' or 'spirit' is, it is something that forms the natural opposite to the body and has less reality value.

If you can try to imagine that your mental universe does not have a concept of something that is 'without substance' then you will find it more possible to understand how the notion of 'more than one body' could exist. Not only were people able to send out a Double of themself, a less dense body that could travel great distances while the other body slept, but they were also able to expel an animal form from their body.

This notion of the animal form has come down to us in modern Traditional Witchcraft as the 'fetch-beast' or 'familiar'. And for those who experienced the presence of one in the past, the animal was believed to be a tangible part of the body that could be expelled through the chest or the mouth of the sleeper and cause literal effects in the world, including being seen by others.

This close connection of the animal self to the person is particularly pronounced in 'were animal' phenomenon, where the person experiences an actual transformation of their physical body into the form of that animal. The real, though highly plastic animal form was able to impose the experience of itself over the experience of being a physical man. So that whilst a scientist would say that the man had not transformed into a beast in his body, a person at the time might have seen a 'man-wolf.'

It is easy to see when we think about this, how the appreciation of something like a werewolf requires at least two people, or preferably a community. It requires a man who experiences his fetch-beast's form over taking his man form, and it requires someone to perceive his beast form as altering the status and meaning of his man-form. Today we seldom have two such individuals in one space to be able to comment on these things that were understood parts of life for our predecessors.

So let us dig a little deeper to try and better understand the older way of seeing the body and soul and the Double that goes forth. In Eva Pocs book *Between the Living and the Dead* she describes how the 'Double' of a person was a believed to possess substance, a literal 'second skin.' As she puts it: 'According to the documentation, the alter ego is imagined to be a physical reality. This means that it was not a soul but a second body; and while it was of a more spiritual nature, it also had physical reality.' [9]

But not all visitations from the dead or travelling witches was a case of this 'second skin', there was also the notion of 'the Shadow.' The term 'Shadow' was in the past applied to the soul that lives on after death and can become detached from the body in dreams or after death. Some records on witchcraft are unusually precise about *what part* of the spiritual complex of a person they are referring to. In one case a woman went into the room 'and there she could not be experienced in her person, she just walked as a Shadow.' Or: 'Not Mrs Moricz herself, but her image walked with me as a Shadow.'

So when it is claimed that something happened 'in the body before the eyes' this may often refer to the second skin that was believed to be tangible. Not all dead people or all sleepers who roamed during their dreams seem to have possessed this second skin or perhaps to have known how to detach it from their other body. The Skin was often given to the witch by a spirit, such as in the case of the gift of an animal form that a witch may henceforth project her Shadow into and go forth.

The revenant (a potent type of ghost) also had this corporeality, something derived subtly from its corpse, which was deactivated if the dead body was destroyed or dismembered. As it was not unusual for the medieval and post medieval person to believe in Shadows and the real occurrence of dreamed events (more on this below) we are hitting upon a crucial point here. This 'second skin' that belonged to the witch, either in the form of a Double of themselves or an animal form, is one of the things that makes the difference between a witches nocturnal adventures and those of the ordinary dreamer. The ordinary dreamer goes forth in Shadow form, something that is generally invisible but may sometimes be perceived by those with The Sight, whereas the witch is able to project the Shadow into forms, as it testified to by the old term 'dressed in forms.'

The expression 'turnskin' makes a lot of sense when one considers that to our forebears this meant the literal donning of another secret Skin. It also helps us to make sense of the notion of witches appearing in 'someone else's form' or 'riding' them. We know revenants were able to use some subtle part of the corpse to send forth a second skin and that this only worked so long as the corpse remained intact. So we can deduce that all humans have such things but that only some humans have the gift of separating it out from the other body during life. We can deduce this because of the large amount of evidence to suggest that witches often stole or borrowed other people's 'Skins' to get about the countryside disguised as them. This may have been simply for revenge or to implicate somebody else other than themselves but the tiring effects of being 'hag ridden' suggest another purpose behind this 'skin taking.' It is likely that sending forth the second skin requires a large power output from the witch and that, therefore, to send the Shadow out to occupy someone else's and use their vitality instead has its advantages. To illustrate this I will present a detailed folkloric account of a witch attempting to 'ride' a man. The story was originally recorded in Appalachian dialect but I've rendered it in standard English:

> I'm doubting if anyone can help me now. But I'm telling you this because when I die, I want you to know what killed me. Now, you know I never believed in witches but I'm afraid a witch is going to make a ghost of me. Every night of my life for the past three months, a witch has come through the keyhole [typical for a Shadow] to my bedroom. She changes me into a horse and puts a bridle on me and leads me outside. Then, she puts her witch saddle on my neck, plaits my mane into stirrups, jumps on my neck and rides as hard as she can till daylight. Then she brings me back to bed all petered out and there's nothing I can do about it.'[10]

This concept of being 'hag ridden' is in fact a form of possession, of a living person by a living person and the notion of riding the second skin allows us to explain the difference between standard dreams and 'big dreams.' We all know that there are some dreams that we have which seem quite insubstantial; our forebears would say that these dreams were true but that we only attended in our 'Shadow.' But those of us who feel called to witchcraft have often had experiences, open eyed experiences, lucid dreams or visions where we feel that we saw with, or were still in, our body. The 'second skin' separating from the physical skin and becoming filled with the Shadow, something that typically feels 'very real', can often explain these experiences of doing seemingly impossible things. It appears, given that the Shadow of a witch is attested over and over again to inhabiting the 'Skin' of other people, that the Shadow is the sentient part and the 'Skin' a kind of vessel.

All of this relates to what we discussed when we spoke of shamanism and ecstasy. The second skin encourages us to view ecstasy as not so much a leaving behind of the bodily life, but an extension of its capacities, a stretching of our sensory experiences into a world of more plastic forms. The older way of seeing does not invite us to slough off the body but instead to loosen and extend our sense of 'what is body' and what its capacities are. We know as modern people that what we call a 'dream' is partly an REM experience that can be detected and mapped by physiological changes in our body and brain waves, we also know that the experience of a dream seems to transcend these facts. There is another dimension, an experiential dimension to the dream without which the other information is incomplete. And thus we come again to speaking of a state that is both embodied and transcendent.

The topic of dreaming should lead us now to consider the importance of the dreaming for our forebears. Our prejudice in favour of 'outer life' over 'inner life' is so pronounced in the West that few people are able to experience the necessary liminality between the two to experience a werewolf, a faerie visitation or to 'meet the Devil' on a highway like Isobel Gowdie did. As Wilby put it:

Anthropological studies have revealed that in cultures where visionary experience is highly valued, it is considered to be as real as the perceptions of normal waking life. Indeed, as anthropologist Jackson Lincoln has observed, in some cases it is regarded 'as having a greater reality value than actual experience.[11]

This is a very important point that Wilby brings to the fore here. We have literally been conditioned since childhood with such phrases as: 'it's just a dream', with the emphasis on 'just' implying that a dream state has a lesser ontological value than a waking one. Such conditioning can take a bit of undoing. In fact it cannot be undone through reason alone. It is only through experience of the Other, and complete reweaving of the psyche through initiatory death and rebirth that such a change can occur. But in a scholarly way Wilby also points out other factors about pre-industrial life that may also have enhanced the conditions for visionary experience.

In the past more time was spent in 'twilight consciousness' rather than in front of televisions or before harsh electric lights. Today most of our time is spent either in light or in total darkness preparing for sleep, and so we tend to experience sleep and wakefulness, two defined states. But our ancestors, particularly in winter when darkness fell very early, spent a large portion of each day by only the light of a flickering fire, with no other entertainment to occupy their imaginations than stories and conversation. It is easy to imagine that spending at least an hour in the evening by the light of only a fire or a candle or two would place one in a 'between state' more frequently. And repetition of stories than contained shared cultural reference points, stories that were believed at some level even though they were fantastical to the modern mind, further blurs the line between the happenings of 'this world' and the Other.

Also, because of shared sleeping areas (often with adults, children and even animals) sleep tended to be broken. In fact most pre-industrial people experience a nights sleep as two separate sleeps of about four hours each with a period of prayer or meditation on dreams in the middle. It is important then that most lucid dreams and intense remembered dream states occur when people are sleeping in a few hour stints rather than deeply asleep all night long. So if we wish to prepare ourselves to enhance our ability to see into the Otherness we can learn from this. We can increase our amount of 'twilight consciousness', we can sleep for shorts periods of time as a purposeful attempt to invoke a lucid state and we can limit our food consumption during this time. All of this will help to bring us closer to the state our ancestors found themselves in on a daily basis.

But what is perhaps most important is that we begin to enhance our appreciation for the dream state. Take dreams seriously. If you have a bad dream, immediately tell someone all the details of it to diffuse its power. If you dream of something fortunate occurring, refrain from speaking of it, lest you diffuse its power. Try to refrain from speaking about dreams in terms of 'true' and 'untrue' dreams. Dreams should instead be seen as possessing different types or depths of truth. No dream or vision is completely unreal, some just have more importance than others. Some have a kind of existence that is shared by only you, and the deeper type, the power-dream, has an existence that can be shared by other entities and even other people. This type is easily as 'real' as daily waking consciousness. In fact the more you begin to think of yourself as a being that has both an inner and outer life that touch each other mysteriously, the more you will come to understand why some pre-industrial people gave priority to what happened in vision and power-dreams, over that of every day waking reality. And how someone was able to say: 'yes I saw him turn into a wolf before my very eyes.'

The Bestiary

For as from the same piece of clay a potter may fashion either a pot or a tile, so the Devil may shape a witch into a wolf or a cat or even a goat, without subtracting from her and without adding to her at all. For this occurs just as clay is first moulded into one, then shaped into another form, for the Devil is a potter and his witches are but clay.

    -Aino Kallas

To begin the process of familiarising ourselves with the territory and figures of the unseen world that our forebears experienced, I have compiled a list of creatures that dwell there. All of the ones I have chosen to include are here because they either were believed to interact with witches in some way, or they actually were embodied humans that performed a certain Otherworldly task.

Alp

The alp is a Germanic incubus or nightmare that presses the chest of the sleeper. Originally it was a kind of elf and perhaps was not always seen so malignantly. The alp usually afflicts women, entering them via their breath like a snake or tendril of mist so that it may 'feed on their dreams.' Some alps like to bring sexual dreams and others nightmares, or mixtures of both. It is significant to note that children may become an alp if a mother needs to use a horse collar to ease the pain during a long childbirth. Also, a child born with a caul or hair on the palms may become an alp. If a woman who is pregnant is frightened by an animal, the child may be born an alp. Stillborn infants are also suspected to return from the grave as alps and torment their family. It was therefore believed that an alp could be the Double of a human being.

Awenyddion

Gerald of Wales provides us with the only record of the *Awenyddion*:

> Among the Welsh there are certain individuals called Awenyddion who behave as if they are possessed... When you consult them about some problem, they immediately go into a trance and lose control of their senses... They do not answer the question put to them in a logical way. Words stream from their mouths, incoherently and apparently meaningless and lacking any sense at all, but all the same well expressed: and if you listen carefully to what they say you will receive the solution to your problem. When it is all over, they will recover from their trance, as if they were ordinary people waking from a heavy sleep, but you have to give them a good shake before they regain control of themselves... and when they do return to their senses they can remember nothing of what they have said in the interval... They seem to receive this gift of divination through visions which they see in their dreams. Some of them have the impression that honey or sugary milk is being smeared on their

mouths; others say that a sheet of paper with words written on it is pressed against their lips. As soon as they are roused from their trance and have come round from their prophesying, that is what they say has happened...

Although this account was gathering in the Middle Ages this notion of an ecstatic shamanistic practice linked with poetry and inspiration (what the Welsh called the Awen) continues up until this seventeenth century account that has much in common with the material here termed 'witchcraft.' Like the *Awenyddion* the poet in question has Awen enter him through the mouth, but this time via a fetch-beast sent to him by a male familiar spirit. This account of the descent of Awen in the form of a hawk is given in a letter to the 17th century antiquary, John Aubrey, from the Welsh poet, Henry Vaughan (1621-1695), who writes:

As to the later Bards, who were no such men, but had a society and some rules and orders among themselves, and several sorts of measures and a kind of lyric poetry, which are all set down exactly in the learned John David Rhees, or Rhesus his Welsh or British grammar, you shall have there, in the later end of his book, a most curious account of them. This vein of poetry they call Awen, which in their language signifies as much as Raptus, or a poetic furore; and in truth as many of them as I have conversed with are, as I may say, gifted or inspired with it. I was told by a very sober and knowing person (now dead) that in his time there was a young lad fatherless and motherless, and so very poor that he was forced to beg; but at last was taken up by a rich man that kept a great stock of sheep upon the mountains not far off from the place where I now dwell, who clothed him and sent him into the mountains to keep his sheep. There in summer time, following the sheep and looking to their lambs, he fell into a deep sleep, in which he dreamed that he saw a beautiful young man with a garland of green leaves upon his head and a hawk upon his fist, with a quiver full of arrows at his back, coming towards him (whistling several measures or tunes all the way) and at last let the hawk fly at him, which he dreamed got into his mouth and inward parts, and suddenly awaked in a great fear and consternation, but possessed with such a vein, or gift of poetry, that he left the sheep and went about the Country, making songs upon all occasions, and came to be the most famous Bard in all the Country in his time.

Beansidhe and Cyhiraeth

A *beansidhe* is a female spirit of Irish origin primarily known for wailing as an omen of death. The word essentially means: 'woman from the mound' and points toward the Underworldly origin of these creatures. A *cyhiraeth* is a very closely related Welsh spirit that does the same thing. Both spirits are known to appear as hags at times, or as 'washer at the ford' figures, washing the shroud of the one who is about to die. These spirits were probably originally a female ancestor or member of the venerated dead, because they tend to be attached to families and only appear when it is time for a member of that family to go over to the Otherness.

Benandanti or 'Good Walker'

Benandanti are a type of ecstatic human who lead a double life as a spirit, in this double existence they fought enemy witches for the benefit of their community and its harvest. They involuntarily left their bodies on the Ember Days (very close to the four fire festivals often practiced in witchcraft today) or on Thursdays. Their flights usually began at the age of eighteen and persisted until they were forty. The term and phenomenon is Italian but the prevalence elsewhere of 'white witches' and cunning men who specialised in counter-magic or protection from witches in many other parts of Europe, Great Britain and the Appalachian Mountains of America, suggests that such a notion might have been more wide-spread initially.

Changeling

A changeling is a faerie that has been exchanged for a mortal child. We need to understand this in the same way we understood the 'change' of the werewolf. Whilst today we would see the same baby lying in the cot and say that only its behaviour had changed, in the past a switch was seen to have occurred. Often these children would go on to have something very wrong with them or even die. Some were considered simple, some were never satiated by human food, others grew up to be relatively normal, but this was usually the exception rather than the rule. Exactly why faeries were in the habit of exchanging their children for human children is not clear, but it points to an inter-penetration and process of exchange with the Otherworld than we commonly no longer perceive today.

Donas de Fuera

A name for faeries in Sicily and also for the women who associated with them. No actual distinction was drawn in their language between the women of faerie and the ostensibly human individuals who joined them in their company. It was believed that through joining them on their rides and for their feasting that good luck and abundance would henceforth rain down on your community, as though they acted as a kind of diplomatic envoy from the human village. The faerie people insisted on there being no mentions of Christ or the Virgin Mary and provided sexual partners to humans.

Faerie/fae

These Siths or Fairies they call Sleagh Maith or the Good People...are said to be of middle nature between Man and Angel, as were Daemons thought to be of old; of intelligent fluidous Spirits, and light changeable bodies (lyke those called Astral) somewhat of the nature of a condensed cloud, and best seen in twilight. These bodies be so pliable through the sublety of Spirits that agitate them, that they can make them appear or disappear at pleasure.[11]

The word 'faerie' like 'witch' has become such a general blanket term that one must make clear what one means by it. A great scope of beings are known as 'faerie' with hell hounds even being described as 'faerie dogs'. But when we use it in relation to witches and sorcery it more often relates to the Shining Court. I do this for disambiguation, because other more 'infernal' types of faeries came to be known in later times simply as 'devils' or 'demons' or by more specific names like 'goblin.' Most 'faerie-seers' or 'faerie-doctors' or 'magicians' behave in a way that is usually benevolent to mankind. I say 'usually' with great emphasis as we are here dealing with a greatly unpredictable entity. And one should also not fall to believing the Christian notion that anything that appears 'dark' or comes from below the earth is necessarily not benevolent, for that matter. Instead one should limit one's assumptions when it comes to encountering Otherworldly beings!

For practical dealing with them it should be noted that the realm of Faerie seems to thrive on contradiction and ambiguity. They love twilight and between times. Stale bread is considered a defence against them and yet bread is often an offering to them. Faeries prefer reciprocation or remembrance of a good deed rather than 'thanks.' They may take offence to being thanked. They also do not like to be given money as a gift or payment for their benevolent behaviour. Iron is a kind of poison to them and most Faeries enjoy milk.

Faerie-Seer or Doctor

A faerie-seer or doctor was an individual who interacted with the realm of faerie and 'doctored' or healed with their assistance. Bessie Dunlop essentially acted as one, though she was tried as a witch. But generally speaking the phenomena was best known in Ireland and Sicily. In Ireland up until the nineteenth century there were still 'faerie- doctors'. Sicily also boasts an entire set of trials known as the 'Sicilian Fairy Trials' that centred around the prosecution of individuals who interacted with faerie. Notable, faerie-based crimes were also on the list of heresies Joan of Arc was charged with. In many cases the 'faerie-doctor' or 'faerie-magician' was actually believed to be faerie themselves, either through having been a changeling or in some other unspecified manner, or simply was 'marked by the faeries.' This is one of the many examples here were the line is blurred between humans and Otherworldly beings.

Lady Wilde described a faerie-seer one who lived in Innis Sark:—

He never touched beer, spirits, or meat in all his life, but has lived entirely on bread, fruit and vegetables. A man who knew him thus describes him—'Winter and summer his dress is the same—merely a flannel shirt and coat. He will pay his share at a feast, but neither eats nor drinks of the food and drink set before him. He speaks no English, and never could be made to learn the English tongue, though he says it might be used with great effect to curse one's enemy. He holds a burial-ground sacred, and would not carry away so much as a leaf of ivy from a grave. And he maintains that the people are right to keep to their ancient usages, such as never to dig a grave on a Monday, and to carry the coffin three times round the grave, following the course of the sun, for then the dead rest in peace.[13]

Furious Horde

Otherwise known as the Wild Hunt this procession of the dead is usually led by a 'Lord of the Dead' figure. In Wales it was Gwyn ap Nudd, sometimes described as 'king of the goblins', or in Germanic areas Odin. Some regions maintained the archaic remnant of a female led infernal procession. Others had both a male and a female leader of the Hunt. The female led hunts were something which many women tried as 'witches' admitted to having participated in. This is another example where mythic entities, the dead, and the Doubles of human witches rubbed shoulders in a way that suggested no fundamental barrier between the dead, Otherworldly beings and living witches.

Ganconagh or 'love talker'

These male faerie creatures were known for seducing young women, and are probably a survival of older lore about a woman's fetch-mate. They were usually first perceived by the girl through a hole in a wall or a hole in a holy stone (an established way of viewing the faerie realm). It is said that he showed the young woman a world of such beauty and wonder that when he left she would simply pine away. Though some Scottish matrons have it that not all such young girls are affected in this way, some go out and 'make something of their life' on account of it. This sounds very much like a form of passage of inspiration, though it is not as clear because women historically didn't have the same opportunities to express inspiration as men. This may make the *Ganconagh* the masculine equivalent of the *Leannan Sidhe*, both are dangerous but potentially give rewards. The *Ganconagh* is associated with smoking a pipe while leaning on a wall or, like the poet's Awen-giving spirit, with making a tuneful whistling as he comes.

Ghost Seers

The women who were sometimes considered 'female benandanti' were able to see the dead. Their role seems to have lain in prediction of death and interceding with the dead on behalf of the living. Sometimes they also attended feasts with the dead or instructed others in how to offer to the dead. The ghost seer's presence in the village ensured that the dead were kept happy and appeased and therefore that things would go right in the community.

A woman named Anna La Rossa is a good example of such seers of the dead. She made a living through plying her ability to talk with those that had passed over, but this skill involved ecstasy like other forms of witchcraft. It came up in her trial that: 'this woman used to be called by her husband many times at night... and even though he elbowed her vigorously, it as if she was dead, because she would say that the spirit had set out on a journey and thus the body was as though dead.''[14] When Anna was out on such sojourns she said that she learned secrets from the dead that she dare not repeat on threat of being beaten with sorghum by them. A female leader who appeared as a nocturnal goddess usually led the processions of the dead that these ghost seers took part in during ecstasy.

Incubus and Succubus

The incubus and succubus were understood as male and female sexually predatory demons. But it seems likely that a great deal of different entities could have easily had their lore find its way under this heading. As with the title 'witch' any entity that engaged in sex with a mortal witch could easily be termed an 'incubus or succubus.' The incubi or succubae were believed to drain their victim's vitality through sexual intercourse and the stealing of the breath. There is far too much lore on the topic to suggest that the element of predation was only invented by the church, it seems clear that this vampiric practice would at times occur. All powers associated with the world of the dead are depicted as being hungry for the vital-force of the living even if only at certain times of the year, and if it is not given as an offering some powers have been known to take it by force and leave blight behind. This being said, the fetch-mate of a witch, a spirit that chooses to unite sexually with them for mutual benefit can often perform a power exchange of types with the human in question. An example of this can be seen under 'Leannan Sidhe.'

Leannan Sidhe

Leannan Sidhe lore is a valuable source of information about reciprocal power exchange between a human and a spirit lover. Whilst the *Leannan Sidhe* is, like the succubus, guilty of draining off the life-force of her human lover, she (or perhaps also at times he) gives in return the fire of inspiration. Whilst this may at times shorten a poet or artist's life span it is inarguably a kind of exchange rather than a straightforward predation. Some of the spirits that we tend to call the blanket term 'fetch-mates' in modern Traditional Witchcraft may belong to this category. Please see the chapter on the fetch-mate for more information.

Lidérc

The *Lidérc* was a creature of Hungarian origin that came in a few different forms. One of them was like an imp, hatched out of the egg of a black hen. But the other more anthropomorphic form bears similarities with the succubus or incubus. It appeared to a woman as a man with horse's hooves and sometimes wings. This form of the *Lidérc* flies at night, appearing as a fiery light, a will o' the wisp, or even as a bird of fire. It was also believed that sometimes the *Lidérc* could be the Double of a human practitioner travelling in animal form or part animal form.

Malandanti

'*Malandanti*' is an Italian word that essentially covers what we think of when we say 'black witch' or a practitioner of maleficium. Had Isobel Gowdie been born in Italy there is a good chance she'd have been known as a 'malandanti' rather than just 'witch.' Like the *benandanti* the *malandanti* were compelled to be as they were, though less information seems to have been collected about how they were marked out and in what manner they were compelled. Whilst the *benandanti* fought with fennel, they fought with or rode on sorghum, something that has a traditional association with the dead, as we can see from Anna La

Rossa's account above. Like the post-witchcraft-trials image of the witch in general, *malandanti* blighted crops, fouled the wine in its kegs, caused infertility and soured milk. In other words they were envoys of a world 'in reverse', of the back-to-front world of the dead.

Mara

The original 'night mare' a very widespread concept with variants such as: Mara/Mare/Mahr/Mora/Morina/Zmora/Morava, in different countries throughout Europe. Even as far as Wales there is a 'spirit of death' figure attested to in folklore known as 'Margan' who may be related to the Mara-complex. These terms all most likely derive from the Indo-European root word *Moros* (death).[15] This feminine entity arguable had more impact on the development of the image of the 'witch' than any other creature. A 'mara' may be either a spirit or may be incarnated as a living human. As Eva Pocs puts it: 'All the peoples of Europe are acquainted with mora creatures that appear exclusively as dead souls – as returning souls – but generally it is clear that the dead moras are the dead variants of those who were mora creatures during their lifetimes.'

The features of the Mora creature vary from place to place, but all are able to send their Double into other people's dwellings, sometimes as an animal or simply as mist. In Slavic countries they are also known as Nocnica or 'night women' or a 'striges'. They sit on the chest and oppress the sleeper, perhaps draining his vital force or 'riding' the sleeper. She was somewhat like a female alp and like the alp a human woman could easily be accused of being a 'mare'. The figure of the 'night woman' or 'mare' is of course where we derive the term 'nightmare'.

Eva Pocs believes that this spirit known for 'riding' the sleeper was the original of the malevolent witch figure and we can see several other features that mora creatures have in common with the later 'witch', for instance, an injury to the animal form or Double will injure the mora. Additionally it was believed that mora-creatures could float on water and not sink. It is this earlier belief that led to the practice of 'swimming' witches to see if they were sink and thus prove themselves innocent.

Mazzeri

The *mazzeri* is a Corsican phenomenon. Like the *benandanti* and *malandanti* the *mazzeri* was also experienced spiritual compulsion. They would turn into a kind of beast, usually something like a black dog and would hunt out those fated to die. If they killed the Double of someone in the Otherworld the person's physical body would soon die here on earth. There is some suggestion that something like the *mazzeri* may have originally been more widely spread. In Wales where the *'cwn annwn'* or hell-hounds were a very important part of folklore the pack of hounds seems to be responsible for rounding up the dead. But there is a different type of hound in Welsh mythology that travels alone. This large black beast, unlike the pack animals, actually stalks and pursues those who are *doomed to die*, there is even suggestion that like the *mazzeri* this solitary hell-hound might have played an active rather than just a predictive role in delivering the message of Fate. As Marie Trevelyan explains in her *Folk-Lore and Folk-Stories of Wales*:

> Sometimes they [solitary spirit dogs] were known to go in pursuit of people who were doomed to die with twelve months from one of the processional nights. Then they went quietly, stealthily... They were seen but not heard as they ran quickly from room to room... in pursuit of their victim. It was stated that on certain occasions the spirits [Doubles] of those pursued people were seen running out into the night followed by the hideous hound.

The main difference between this Welsh spirit dog and the mazzeri, is that the mazzeri was explicitly known to also live in the form of a human male or female who had a second skin in the form of a dog.

The mazzeri tended to believe that they were carrying out a fateful edict rather than simply killing people. In their communities they were considered useful because they were often able to warn people of impending death. Their very existence hints at the way human 'witches' have been called upon to aid in Otherworldly processes and how we human witches often form necessary 'points of interaction' between this world and the next. Through us certain tensions are discharged, through us certain hungers are appeased, through us certain Fate messages are passed along. In it all the human witch, whether faerie-doctor or mazzeri or even malandanti is simply 'marked' and has little choice but to perform this function on behalf of greater powers. There is evidence, however, that the experienced ecstatic could come to influence *how* and upon whom they performed their function, which we will come to later.

Revenant

To understand the revenant one must already understand what we have said about the corporeal nature of the soul. Lecouteux's work on revenants in *The Return of the Dead* has done a great deal to correct our understanding of the potential of ghosts. A 'revenant' is usually a kind of ghost that has failed to complete a crucial life transition, and thus still has a great deal of vital force untapped. This vital force allows the second skin to continue to live on after death. It may even prevent the physical body from decaying for a while, as it uses it as its base from which to conduct its new life. Revenants are able to be seen and to affect their environment in certain ways. The only way to get rid of one is via the body, it must either be dismembered in some way or moved too far away that it is unable to travel back to its home because revenants find it difficult or impossible to stray too far from their body.

Snake Man

A Serbian, Bulgarian and Macedonian phenomenon the *zmajevit covek*, snake-men or snake-magicians, were born with cauls that looked like snakeskins over their faces or even literal snakeskin over them. Many were said in addition to their reptilian characteristics to have secret wings, usually of an eagle. These allowed them to participate in supernatural flight. When a storm with hail in it was approaching they fell into trances and fought fiery battles using lightning against darker, watery serpents that brought destructive storms.[16] There is some evidence that this phenomenon might have once been wider spread, as Welsh folklore contains a lot of information about snake-people and also about sightings of winged serpents.

Táltos

The Hungarian *táltos* could be either male or female, but were more often than not, men. They were born with more bones than the unusual, like six fingers (altogether 11 or 12 fingers) or already-grown-in teeth or a long head of hair. *Táltos* were believed to be 'born knowing' having been tutored in their future role in the pre-natal phase by spirits or gods. They did not need to learn how to perform their role. At some point they would meet the 'táltos horse' that only they would be able to ride, and thus they would learn to fly through the skies in the Otherworld.

Erzsébet Balázsi, a *táltos*, was accused of being a witch. The court asked her to explain the role of *táltos*. She said: the *táltos* cures, sees buried treasures with the naked eye, and 'the *táltos* are fighting for Hungary in heaven'. So it is clear to see from this that the benevolent role of the *táltos* makes it similar to the *benandanti*, though the *táltos* was marked by precociousness and more extreme physical differences. When the *táltos* did battle with enemy practitioners they would usually turn into a stallion, a bull or a ball of flame.

Were-beasts

Folklore provides us with examples of other 'were' people that were known for transforming into animals other than wolves, and where this tendency was even believed to be in the family. In Wales there were believed to be a 'fox clan' whose members had red-hair who would turn their Skin to their fox form at the Midsummer Solstice and the Midwinter one.

There were also people who were known for turning into snakes. These traditions must hark back to the days when families would share the same animal-form or pass it on to their children. The 'purpose' of these transformations seems to have been to allow the individual to partake of the powers of that animal, such as the cunning of the fox, but whether there was more to their function, as with the werewolf, this is for the time being unknown.

Werewolves

Werewolves underwent a great transformation at the hands of the witch-hunter. The information coming to us directly from men who claimed to be werewolves depicts their role entirely differently than the diabolical image we have been led to believe. The famous werewolf Thiess, insisted at some length in his trial that werewolves are not evil, they did in fact go down into Hell to steal back the grains and other needfuls that the people of the Underworld (with the help of witches) had stolen from the world above. But Thiess is not the only example of the 'benevolent' werewolf.

In the mid-sixteenth century an anecdote about a young man of Riga was recorded. He had suddenly fallen prostrate during a banquet and one of the onlookers had been able to immediately tell that he was a werewolf. The next day the youth related that he had fought a 'witch' who had been flying around as a red-hot butterfly. Werewolves apparently boasted that they kept bad witches away.[17]

This being said, whilst the werewolf believed they were the 'hounds of god' who defended the community they did so by going outside of it. They shed their human clothes and identity and went out past the barriers of things. They became the animal that was most feared by the community inside the hedge for it's ability to predate on humans. Even the term 'wolf' in Saxon times referred to an outlaw, one who had been cast out and had lost the sanctified status of those things within the defined walled or hedged area of the communities allotment. As such the figure of the werewolf was one of ultimate ambiguity, one of a man forced to come very close to the raw and wild forces of the Outside and to face the challenge of reigning them to utilise for the good.

It is noted by Eva Pocs that the dates that were traditional for werewolf transformation were also times traditional for the return of the dead. She notes: 'They also have close relationships with the returning dead and where thought to become active during the periods of the festivals of the dead. Dead, demonic werewolves can also be seen as guardians that attack or protect their tribes.' In this way the werewolf is much like a male version of the mora-creature, in that is seems to start its career as a human who transforms into a wolf and to return later as a dead spirit as well, and thus gain an association with the dead. Like all of the dead this returning wolf may be either helpful or baneful depending on how it has been treated and appeased.

Witch

As we have stated above 'witch' is an infinitely complex word. It is, essentially a blanket term that was thrown over all manner of ecstatic and magical practitioners. And yet by blanketing in this manner a new reality was created. It is noteworthy that some *benandanti* actually refused to name the 'witches' or *malandanti* that they fought against. Although they were enemies the concept of Fate allows us to see both their actions as necessary parts of a whole. Those like Isobel Gowdie who dealt death have been shown to behave, as Emma Wilby has shown, like 'a Fate.'

Whilst the word 'witch' was usually used by some of the types of ecstatics we've mentioned here to denote an enemy, we have seen from the entry on werewolves how subjective the positioning of 'outside the hedge' can be. Regardless of whether one means harm or help the very fact of crossing the hedge makes the ecstatic an outsider in some way.

Some societies were flexible enough to have institutions in place to either embrace or tolerate such aberrance. But regardless of what a *benandanti* might like to think about himself or a werewolf might claim about his actions today's society, as with the Christian world of the past, does not have such a place in its bosom for those born to experience ecstatic episodes and bring back Otherworldly materials. For this reason the word 'witch' with all its connotations of the outside, the back to front and even the sinister, can still be meaningful to a wide range of modern ecstatic practitioners.

Valkyrie

Valkyrie refers to female spirits of Norse origin, the word means 'chooser of the slain'. Unlike the Irish *beansidhe* or the Welsh *cyhiraeth* the valkyrie actually chooses who is to die in battle. In this way the valkyrie performs a function between the worlds that is more like the *mazzeri*, in that they actually deliver the blow of the Fate. Like the valkyrie the *mazzeri* was sometimes also a 'chooser of the slain', being able to occasionally direct the blow of Fate away from a loved one and onto some other unfortunate. The interesting difference here is that the valkyrie was explicitly an Otherworldly woman, whereas the mazzeri was also a mortal woman or man.

This being said the valkyrie did interact with this world in more ways than carrying off the slain, as they were sometimes known to be the lovers of mortal men. They are also listed among 'harmful female spirits' in prayers of protection, where they find their way in beside *'haegtessa'* or 'hedge-riders' another term for witch. Here we see further evidence of the hazy space between the spirit-doings of the human participant and those of non-human Others.

Vampire

The original idea behind 'vampire' was a particular kind of witch possessing 'two hearts' a human one and that of a 'demonic' intelligence. In some places werewolves were also considered to be 'two hearted' in this manner. Both creatures could be identified by extra sets of teeth. During life this person might fly in spirit and feed on the vital force of others and cause milk to sour and crops to fail like the typical 'black witch' or *malandanti*. But after death, like an alp or mara, if such a person was not properly disposed of they may create a revenant and become a blood-seeking member of the living dead. In other areas they were believed to strictly be undead creatures. A vast number of entities of all types could be considered 'vampiric', including the succubus and incubus.

Conclusion

One thing that becomes clear when we combine the information from the Bestiary with our ancient and modern testimonials is that some things change and some things remain. The modern people who provided me with these testimonials did so, in most cases, without realising quite how closely some of their material matched with the older material. The modern witch with the black dog transformation, for instance, had never heard of the *mazzeri*.

But what I think is just as important for us to pay attention to is the differences between the older and the modern material. Ecstatic practitioners like the Hungarian *táltos* and Corsican *mazzeri* were deeply culturally imbedded in their local context. To look at it from an occult rather than a sociological angle, we might say that certain spirit-entities had long standing connections with particular human populations. This meant that those connections tended to play out in a more predictable manner. When that connection was maintained the táltos could reliably be born with a sixth finger or early dentation and a *benandanti* could be reliably be expected to be born with a caul.

Today with these relationships disturbed and dispersed and bloodlines no longer tied to one landscape things are thrown into chaos. But this is not to suggest that the powers have ceased to try to interact with us or even to deny the creative function of chaos. It seems that in being forced down those powers erupt more unpredictably today. Whereas once certain 'marks' could be predicted with certainty, today a caul may or may not signify that spirits will come for that child and it may tell us nothing about which spirits will come, if any do.

Today the modern witch is very much a stranger in a new way, functioning in a strange land where the meaning of their call or their mark is not known or recognised. But really this chaos is simply another manifestation of the unruly forces of the Other, powers from beyond the hedge forcing their way in and pouring through the cracks. What has been lost is not our ability to make contact with those forces, but is instead the systems that were once in place to order them in society. Even the unpleasant persecution of people with certain marks because they were considered 'evil witches' was a form of ordering and dealing with the powers of the Other. So it is important to realise that not all of the ways of 'dealing with' these powers meant integration, some meant outright rejection.

Modern witches who attempt to regather some of these Threads, by bringing together the stories of modern people who experience eruptions of Otherworldly powers, along with the older stories of witchcraft, are in fact trying to write a new narrative of integration. This 'narrative of integration' will not only allow us to position ourselves in relation to others like us, but in relation to the Otherworldly forces that work through us, and in relation to a wider society.

Becoming Yourself

It [witchcraft] can and does embrace the totality of human experience from birth to death, and then beyond. It creates within the human spirit a light that brightens all darkness, and which can never again be extinguished. It is never fully forgotten, it is never fully remembered. The True Faith is the life of the follower, without it he is nothing, with it he has contained something of all creation.
  -Robert Cochrane

For some who find themselves 'marked as Other' it may only be necessary to read of a fetch-beast or animal familiar and immediately you will know that you have one and what it is. For some it is as simple as remembering some very real seeming dreams they used to have. One modern witch has this to say about her experiences of animal transformation:

The first time I dreamed I was other than a human being was one of the most vivid 'dreams' I've ever had. At the same time, it was fragmented and there seems to be pieces missing from my memory. I only dreamed it once, and I was about fourteen when I did.

The first thing that I recall was jumping from my bedroom window, out onto the front lawn. Then I ran very quickly down the street. Everything seemed normal, but it was quite bright, though I knew it was night. I saw the neighbour's house, I saw my house, and I felt like I could run really quickly. The next thing I recall is standing above the remains, or half devoured body of some small furry thing, and I realised I was eating it. Though this didn't disturb me at all. When I looked down at the 'kill' I saw myself, well, part of myself, either side were my hands, except they were not my hands, they were very large paws of a canine. And I remember thinking how awesome it was that I was a wolf! A great big grey-blue wolf. And I bound off down the street again. And that is all I remember. The wolf is the animal form of my fetch-mate (and of my forefather), and though I have memories of dreams in which I interacted with my fetch mate, I didn't take the wolf form again until many years later.

Others may feel that they have experienced some kind of call but have no idea what their familiar powers might be. Although the extended self often manifests in an animal form, as you can see from the examples so far, there is no reason to believe that this will always be the case. So to begin with we will look at the fetch-beast and ways to discover if you have one, and if so, what form it takes.

Fetch-Beast and Familiars

Also called in Germanic tradition the 'Fylgia', the fetch is the follower or guardian that often appears in animal form. In the North it is clear that the Fylgia was inherited, an ancestral being, carrying on the person's behalf the 'luck force' of their family. Most people only saw the fetch close to the time of their own death, but some people were born with a particular gift for 'sending the fetch.'

In general the fetch in its animal form suits the power of that individual and family line, a brave warrior is likely to have a fierce animal. Today most of us have no idea what the fetch-beasts of our family line might have been. And it is also possible that more than one line, or Thread, will express itself through us. This could result in more than one animal familiar. When we look at the prevalence of imps in the witch-trials we see that many witches were able to transform into numerous different types of animals or send them as helpers. And that there were even forms that the whole coven had the ability to turn into at once, such as crows, hares or cats. This being said when someone is in the habit of actually transforming into the beast there is usually a primary animal form, because the beast is part of the second skin of that individual. It is stirred up from inside the body of that person. Though of course the fetch can and does range far from the body of the individual, giving us a hint as to how mysterious and plastic our 'bodies' actually are. Unless a witch has already been chosen by an anthropomorphic spirit familiar in his or her early days this is the first and most important contact that a Witch should make before purposely undertaking to cross the hedge into the unseen.

The reason for this is that the fetch-beast, being connected to us via the body and blood by its nature wants us to survive. It is deeply connected to the animal drive to 'survival and prosper' in us. This cannot be said for all entities that may approach you. So the fetch-beast, or in its place the ancestral guardian or Fate-woman if such a guardian comes forward first (or guardian or Fate-woman who sometimes appears in the form of an animal) is the touchstone against which the safety of all other encounters is measured and double-checked. It is this creature or being whose opinion you will ask when taking future steps with other spirits, because although it is an extension of our own Skin or we of its, its knowledge and power also goes beyond those bounds. As we progress we will see that some of the tools for communicating with the fetch-beast are things you might already be used to listening to, such as the hairs on the back of your neck, and things that you feel 'in your guts' or bones and even the womb and other body parts.

The animal form immediately tells you much about the type of power the animal has. The nature of anything possessing stings, such as a wasp or scorpion, can immediately be known to be hostile and something we should not interact with for now. There are of course exceptions to this, such as when that creature emerges from your mouth or chest as your obvious Double!

The fetch-beast is usually a mammal or bird, (though snakes are also common) and is more often a wild rather than a tame animal, though plenty of horses, cats and dogs crop up in witch-craft trial records. The creature usually, but not always, will belong to a land one has an ancestral connection with or the land in which one was born. The spirit of Monkey, for instance, would seldom emerge from the body of a British person, but the spirit of Kangaroo may well emerge through a sixth generation Australian or someone with Aboriginal blood, for whom the connection between land and body has become deep and intimate over time.

Devils, Familiars and Fetch-brides

A savage place! As holy and enchanted
As e'er beneath a waning moon was haunted
By woman wailing for her demon-lover!
   -Coleridge

As we can see when we look over the testimonies of witches from earlier times not everyone is initially approached by an animal spirit. Isobel Gowdie seems to have initially been approached by 'the Devil', Bessie Dunlop by a faerie man who claims to have once lived as a human man, others were taken by faeries or by the spirit of another living practitioner. So let us now examine the humanoid familiar. These do not really fall into neat categories but for the sake of ease we will simplify the things into three segments. Those who take an interest in the witch due to ancestry or other loyalty, those who take a sexual/romantic interest in the witch and those who are of a higher level of power (the 'Devil', the faerie King or Queen etc).

Fore-parents and Fate-women

The non-sexual humanoid patron includes a wide-range of entities, but usually these patrons are connected to familial relations. They are either, like the fetch, an ancestral patron, or an entity that identifies itself as part of your 'spirit family' or tribe. These spirits will usually function as guides and teachers or they may appear to give fateful messages at important cross-roads in life. Spirits may also become a patron for reasons of sorcerous lineage rather than physical. Such as in cases where witches would see the Doubles of witches known to be dead come for them to initiate them.[18]

Here is a testimonial of a modern day witch, from among my informants, that shows an ancestral familiar or dead family member returning to 'mark' the descendent for sorcery:

Directly in front of me was a cliff, a mountain. I could see on the flat top of the mountain, and there was a fire and a figure standing by it. I would climb up the cliff face that always seemed to be very easy in my dream, because I never felt tired when I reached the top. It was scary and I recall looking back down from where I can and could see down to blackness, as if the place I had been standing had dropped away to nothing and I had to keep going up. I could see out though, over my house, and the houses of my grandparents and other people I knew. When I reached the top there was snow all over the ground. There was an older women standing by a fire and she smiled and held her arms open to me, and I ran to her, and I called out "Grandma!" Though she was not my Grandma that I knew in life and who lived still at this time. When I reached her she hugged me tight and I hugged her back and I said to her in a childish way one does when they are young "I climbed up so far!" and she smiled at me. She wore a big coat that seemed to be able to wrap right around me and felt very warm in the snow. And she said the same thing every time "Welcome home, I've been waiting for you. Its time for you to come home." She would turn and gesture for me to look out over the land from which the mountain rose. All the houses were gone and there were forests that seemed to go on forever and far away I could see the ocean. And then I would wake abruptly. Whenever I woke I was disappointed and I would try to go back, trying desperately to fall asleep. But I always woke from the dream at the same moment, and the women would always say the same thing to me, and I never once was able to get back.

I was much older before I saw this woman again in this manner. She is my foremother, my Mother's Grandmother, and I call her Far Mor, as my Mother always did. And I see her in trance and in spirit flight. I have walked with her in that forest and I have sat with her in the mountain. And I understand now that this is the home of my Ancestors in the Otherworld, and her fur coat and fireside is always waiting for me when I return.

Fetch-Mate or Faerie Lover

Another frequent type of familiar is the fetch-mate, who in the past was known as succubus or incubus by the church because of their propensity to mate with the human witch. This kind of Otherworldly marriage scenario seems to be quite widespread amongst witches in the past, modern witches and also shamans of other cultures.

The first witch to go on record as having an 'incubus' who had carnal knowledge of her was Alice Kyteler of Ireland who lay with her familiar Robin Artisson.

Later in the history of the persecution of witchcraft we find the sexual intercourse theme continuing, but usually being recorded as occurring between the witch and 'the Devil'. Many have argued that this is a preoccupation in the minds of the inquisitors, but as Emma Wilby and others like Graham Hancock [19] have shown this theme of marriage and intercourse with a spirit is common among other shamanic peoples around the world. This being said the inquisitors certainly made it difficult sometimes to get at the true spiritual core of the experience. On one occasion the spirit was even recorded as being 'the Devil' when a male witch outright told the inquisitor that his female spirit lover was the Queen of faerie! Usually we hear little about the nature of the sexual relations with the human familiar. We do, however, hear that the faerie witches of Sicily were offered handsome men to have sex with and we hear of other male witches who obtained their powers through an intimate moment with an Otherworldly female, the first from the 1600's the other from the 1100's:

The first example, recorded by Nicholas Remy, is of a herdsman found guilty of witchcraft who, when asked how he had first fallen into the company of witches, explained that he had been seduced by a succubus. The herdsman said that he had fallen passionately in love with a dairymaid who did not return his affections. One day, he was, in his own words, 'burning with desire in his solitary pasturage' when he saw what at first he took for the person of his beloved hiding behind a bush. He ran to her and made violent advances, and was repulsed. After a while, the 'dairymaid'- in reality, a demon who had assumed the girl's appearance- allowed the herdsman to do with her body as he would on condition that he 'acknowledged her as his Mistress, and behaved to her as though she were God Himself'.

The second example, recorded by Gerald of Wales in the Middle Ages, is similar in that it begins with the man seeing his beloved and trying to couple with her:

It is worthy of observation, that there lived in the neighbourhood of this City of Legions, in our time, a Welshman named Melerius, who, under the following circumstances, acquired the knowledge of future and occult events. Having, on a certain night, namely that of Palm Sunday, met a damsel whom he had long loved, in a pleasant and convenient place, while he was indulging in her embraces, suddenly, instead of a beautiful girl, he found in his arms a hairy, rough, and hideous creature, the sight of which deprived him of his senses, and he became mad. After remaining many years in this condition, he was restored to health in the church of St. David's, through the merits of its saints. But having always an extraordinary familiarity with unclean spirits, by seeing them, knowing them, talking with them, and calling each by his proper name, he was enabled, through their assistance, to foretell future events.

Here we see two female fetch-brides (one probably in a half fetch-beast half anthropomorphic form, judging by the description of 'rough and hairy') skilled at working through the 'second skin' of the human beloved and utilising that desire to draw the male witch towards consummation and subsequently 'infecting' him with, or perhaps just awakening him, to his Otherworldly vocation.

There are other examples of partly bestial encounters between witches and their spirit lover where the line between fetch-beast and fetch-mate seems to blur. The *liderc* was one such creature, who frequently appeared with horses hooves, similarly to the Devil himself who was often described as having a cloven hoof. And the witch Margaret Lauder claimed that '(her devil) came and lay with her in a beastly manner while her back was toward him.'

Just like shamans in other countries who experience reproductive experiences with their spirit brides or husbands Andro

Man of Aberdeen, Scotland impregnated his faerie bride with numerous children over the years. 'Andro Man appears to have been the husband of the Queen of Elphen, with whom he had lived for thirty-two years and by whom he had several children."[20]

What follows are some testimonial from modern witches about their experience of the fetch-mate or faerie lover:

There were times on these nights I dreamt of mating with my fetch-beast. Sometimes we were both dogs. Sometimes she was human but I not. Other times we were both human. Sometimes we would both be something in between. It was carnal and potent and horrific and awe inspiring all at the same time.

    -male witch

It was always quite clear to me that the spirit man who came to me all my life took a romantic interest in me. But it wasn't until well into my twenties that he initiated a sexual encounter with me. The first time I was in a half sleep state and had a very tactile sensation of him, a cool, tingly sort of feeling. As time has gone along my strongest encounters with him have been in lucid dream states and visions where he seems to ejaculate fire into me. Knowledge, light and beautiful images are passed between us via our foreheads. Sometimes he changes his shape but I always know it's him. He can communicate with me without talking at this time and sometimes he shows me the world through his eyes and will look through mine.

    -modern witch

When I am with my fetch-mate in the Otherworld he is very much a man. I do not experience him as cold or hot, but he is wholly solid. During sex with him it is not uncommon for him to shift back and forth from man to wolf, sometimes both at the same time. We bite each other a lot at when I feel him bite me even if he appears as a man I feel as if the teeth are the wolf's. Often sex is initiated when we are both in wolf form and its generally very aggressive, almost like fighting. When 'climax' is reached though it is not like a normal experience. There isn't a 'him' or a 'me' and there seems to be almost complete formlessness between us. Visually I feel like I am inside a fire, but I am also part of that fire. Afterwards it is like a 'settling' back into form. I do not know that we speak at this time, and for the most part there is an over whelming energy exchange and I feel very empowered after. After interactions like this I find I have the most vivid dream visions and often answers to questions are revealed to me in this way. I sleep very soundly, but I have a heightened ability to recall dreams and visions.

When he comes to me here it's different, but ultimately has the exact same effect in reverse. Sex is like an offering to him of my vital force and I find as I reach climax I have experience of him touching me or grabbing me. At this time he feels cold, and though I am surprised how I feel him, he is not solid to me as he is in the Otherworld. He becomes increasing clear to me though, and especially I can hear him, and though I am in control physically, he does tell me what he wants, and what I should do. Often as I reach climax am shocked suddenly by the feeling of being entered by him. At these times I sort of have internal vision of him, and myself together in the room, as if I have his perspective as well. After I feel physically drained and he seems to be always encouraging me to eat something, His voice and presence in my home after is very strong, and I find I am able to talk with him for a long time, I can take notes, and write things down, but I find spirit flight very difficult after this.

-Female witch

But the spirit who approaches an individual is not always of the opposite sex, as can be seen from the example of the poet who's inspiration is recorded under the entry 'Awenyddion.' Other than this spirit sending a hawk to enter the poet's body there is nothing amorous in the normal way about this encounter, other than the man's recollection that he was 'beautiful', but today, freed somewhat from the persecutions and prejudices of the past we find that the romantic spirit mate does not always appear as a spirit of the opposite sex.

> *I know my fetch [mate]. I've known my fetch [mate] before I knew what that even meant. Even after I knew what a fetch was, I still had no idea that I'd already been in contact, because I was looking for an exclusively female being. I've dreamed about him, some man that knows me and I know him, even though I don't see his face (but at the same time, I do). He shows me things that are useful in the everyday and shares secrets. He then somehow places that skill inside of me so that I can take the skill with me outside of this dream and then we had sex. One time, he appeared to me as me. I was looking at me, but I recognized him. Again, we have 'sex'. I use 'quotes' because I don't think it was physical sex, more like to psychedelic ribbons wrapping around each other like DNA?*
> -Male witch

Once again it is clear between older and more modern sources that these encounters range from ethereal and 'psychedelic' to intensely primal, that the spirit is usually but not always of the opposite sex, and may mix human and animal characteristics, or change his/her shape regularly. It is clear that these spirits take an active interest in the sorcerous cultivation of the witch, as sex almost always involves the regular transference of 'fire' or power to the human witch.

This transference of fire is linked to the very deepest mysteries that relate to our origins and the reason why these spirits seek to know humans. Sexual visitations have also been known to be sent by a sleeper to another living human, such as with the Alp and the Mara. Female witches have even been known to appear 'in the Double of' a man known to them to 'sexually harass' another sleeping female. Though how it was known that it was not the man who it appeared to be is uncertain!

Amorous Devils:

This Serpent, Satan is not the enemy of man, but he who made gods of our race, knowing Good and Evil...
　　-Aleister Crowley

The 'devil' is said to appear at the crossroads, near a gallows or on a lonely highway, and to have many disguises. Folklore makes it clear that you can never really trust him, and yet the Scots tell us: 'the Devil is good to his own.' Modern Traditional Witchcraft worships him as The Master under many names. It is said of him that it is He who gave the gift of cunning fire to mankind (or at least led the way among other important spirits who also did so); the fire that brings forth mankind's artfulness, that marks humans as different from the other animals, and also allows for the possibility of sorcery.

But his ways are complex and mercurial and as such he has been more abused, of late, in history than he has been worshipped. With the narrative of Christianity having gained so much power, to truly understand him we often need to take power back from this so dominant story. And when we do there are witches who will say that our Master is both Jesus and Lucifer, he is both rebellious goat and sacrificial lamb, and for his ambiguity at every level, he is reviled by society. He is Jesus about to be crucified and he is Judas the betrayer who gives Jesus up to be crucified.

To witches he is sometimes also known through the apocryphal Christian traditions and named Azazel the fallen Watcher, lover and teacher of sorcery to human women, the divine-smith who turns and shapes the metal of our souls until they are strong and sharp and able to endure. It is perhaps these other 'Watchers' that followed Azazel in his interest in the 'daughters of man' that might give us a clue as to the meaning behind the love between the human witch and the daimonic fetch-mate.

And yet when we reach for Him in the way the witches of old might have seen him we cannot only deal with the Christian gloss, for there were native traditions at work also. It is interesting to note that the word 'devil' in Scotland became almost synonymous with the more neutral term 'spirit.' This is well illustrated in the still common saying: 'oh you poor wee devil', which is simply a way of saying: 'you poor soul.' So, whilst the inquisitors saw all spirits that the witches dealt with as 'the Devil', what they in fact interacted with was 'the devil' or 'the spirit' of their coven. Each area that covenanted with a 'devil' of this kind worked with a local avatar or representative of the Master. This relationship was intimate in many cases, with the devil having sexual relations with all of his female witches. This makes sense considering the association between Azazel and the fallen Watchers both laying with and teaching witchcraft to human women.

We also hear from Isobel Garcia in the Basque region a tale suggesting that the Devil himself was sometimes fond of intercourse with his male as well as his female witches.[21] And Isobel Gowdie, though primarily mentioning the women in her coven having sex with their devil does say of her mixed-sex coven that the devil would lie with 'any and all.' There is little other evidence of the Devil behaving in this manner, though Michael Erskine of Scotland in 1613 was found guilty of witchcraft and sodomy as part of a co-joined crime, though there is no further information with whom this was performed. Usually when a man obtained an important connection with 'the Devil' it was through the medium of a female figure, as happened for Andro Man with the Queen of faeries and the angel/devil Christsonday. Otherwise for men the focus of any sexual union with deities was simply a faerie woman or the faerie Queen herself. The faerie Queen was not quite as well known for her amorous pursuit of human men as the Devil was with women, but the stories are certainly there. Andro Man claims to have fathered children by her and Thomas the Rhymer became romantically entangled with her.

Congress with the Devil became a popular part of sabbat mythology, but testimonies like the vivid one of Isobel Gowdie suggest that we cannot write this off as merely the exaggeration of the interrogators. There are simply too many details here that an interrogator would never think to enquire about, Isobel has provided more than a simple answer to a question: 'yes I copulated with the Devil', she provides us with a rich narrative of the experience. Here is Isobel's testimony about sex with their coven's devil, rendered in modern English:

The next time I met with him was at Inshoch, and he had carnal copulation and dealings with me, he was a great black man [was black, had black hair or was dressed in black, this is unclear in the usage of the time] who felt very cold. His penis and semen were as cold inside me as well water. Sometimes he had boots on sometimes his cloven hoof was visible. When he has carnal copulation with me he feels as heavy laying upon me as a malt-sack. His member is exceedingly great and long and no man's member is so large as his is. At sabbats he would come among us like a stallion among mares and he would lie with us in front of everyone. Neither he nor we had any kind of shame about this, but he especially is shameless. He would lie with all and any that he pleased and he would sometimes copulate with us in the form of a stag or other shape that he would turn into and we would never refuse him. He would come to my house in the shape of a crow, or a stag and any other shape and then I would know his voice at the first hearing of it and would go forth with him and have sex with him. The youngest and lustiest women experienced a lot of pleasure in copulation with him, more so than with their husbands and they had exceedingly great desire of it with him, as much as he would provide them with and more. And they never felt ashamed of it. He was far more able in this department than any man can be (alas that he should even be compared to a mortal man!) except for the fact of how heavy he felt and how cold his member/semen felt.[22]

The Crossroads Pact

Shall we write about the things not to be spoken of?
Shall we divulge the things not to be divulged?
Shall we pronounce the things not to be pronounced?
  - Julian, *Hymn to the Mother of the Gods*

The concept of a pact, particularly one with the Devil is a relative latecomer to witchcraft mythology.[23] Early examples of magical grimoires such as the *Greek Magical Papyri* and even the *Key of Solomon* both present the occultist as 'master of spirits', just as the tribal shaman is in traditional cultures. In fact the *Greek Magical Papyri* actually shows the mage extracting an oath of allegiance from the daimon, rather than the other way around! It seems to be a uniquely post-Christian idea that the witch obtained his or her power from a pact with the devil or other powerful familiar. But before we reject the practice outright it might pay to take apart some of the motifs within it to find if, like so many other witchcraft traditions, there is something of an elder power hiding behind the diabolism.

The first and most obvious example of a pre-Christian trace is in the motif of the crossroads. The idea of 'selling your soul at the crossroads' took on particular power in the New World and has a large part in the history of jazz in the South. But the importance of the crossroads doesn't just belong to the afro-Caribbean strain of magic in the new world, but to European magic as well. Alice Kyteler in Ireland as far back as the thirteenth century sacrificed black cocks to her demon/familiar Robin Artisson at a crossroads, and of course the large amount of gallows based sorcery (corpse necromancy, the hand of glory etc) is linked to the crossroads and to Odin as god of sorcery. So clearly we can see that the location of the crossroads as a place at the centre of things and therefore neither here nor there has an ancient power. If one wished to meet with spirits going to a crossroads would indeed make sense. It is also possible that the 'trampling on the cross' that witches are accused of was a piece of ritual equipment symbolic of the crossroads, rather than a purely heretical act.

The second factor that comes to mind is the abjuration of the Christian baptism by the witch. This is perhaps one of the most important points to be said for the idea of pacts. Just because something is post-Christian does not mean it is without occult value. It may actually address a new need that was not present in former eras. If a spiritual ritual of baptism has been performed on you as an infant before you could consent you may well wish to confirm your status as one 'outside' by renouncing this ritual formally. This renunciation can be done by saying the Lord's Prayer backwards, in essence 'unsaying' one's allegiance to the Christian god, or it can simply be written into the verbal agreement of the pact that you 'abjure and reject all previous allegiances particularly those formed without your consent in infancy.'

The next thing that usually happened is blood was drawn

from the candidate in the process of making the 'mark.' It is difficult to say whether this is something that was invented by the witch hunters or not. As we have said previously the idea of a 'mark' is unlikely to have originally been something that was etched or drawn on the person by the Devil. The folklore from which the idea came probably referred to inborn factors. However the drawing of blood is intriguing, particularly in Isobel Gowdie's case where she stipulates that the devil of their coven 'sucked the blood from her shoulder', this hints at the kind of power transfer between humans and spirits that will be discussed in more detail in 'The Suckling Imp.'

The pact may then be signed with the witch's blood and thus her soul is transferred to the Devil and she likely will also be expected to keep the secrets she is shown. It is noteworthy that secrecy in relation to what sorcery one is performing is mentioned among the most ancient written sources we have on the topic. Originally this seems to have served the practical purpose of 'keeping in the power' whereas talking about an operation would diffuse that power. But later in a time of persecution there was a new impetus to remain silent.

Another common motif is for the witch to kneel down and offer 'all that is between the hands' to the spirit. It is likely that this practice also has it's roots in folklore, as there is an example of faerie-seers who in no way saw themselves as in league with the Devil, placing their hands above the head and the foot of the someone and in this way allowing the person to 'see with their faerie Sight.' The one hand above the head and one under the foot was probably originally a way of sponsoring a person into 'seeing' with the Other Eye and became co-opted into a diabolical framework by the inquisitors. Here is an example of a similar practice being used to pass the second sight from a faerie-seer to someone that doesn't have it in the 1600's.

The usual method for a curious person to get a transient sight of this otherwise invisible crew of subterraneans is to put his left foot under the wizard's right foot, and the seer's hand is put on the inquirer's head, who is to look over the wizard's right shoulder (which has an ill appearance, as if, by this ceremony an implicit surrender were made of all betwixt the wizard's foot and his hand ere the person can be admitted a privado [an initiate] to the Art.[24]

This quote shows that not only did the author associate this posture with initiation by this period but that people who did not consider themselves to be evil or in league with the Devil certainly used the posture that became associated with 'giving all between these two hands to the Devil.' It is also noteworthy to mention that it is the left (receptive) foot that the person places under the right (active) foot of the recipient. This can give us clues to performing this act effectively.

So what do we have when we bring all this together? We have a location that confounds all either/or definitions and is the place of total ambiguity. We have the renouncing of the 'magic' that was done to the person to keep them wholly and solely with the flock and inside the hedge. This is undone and then a kind of power sharing is undertaken between a human and a spirit. The spirit gives them 'fire' and the witch gives them vital force, or a sacrifice of vital force from a slaughtered cock, in return.

Often the true nature of this pact is revealed by it being followed by carnal intercourse. It is thus revealed that what is happening here is not a selling of the soul so much as a distorted memory of a marriage ceremony. Just as in a marriage the parties promise certain things to each other and forsake certain others. The process might involve being 'given away' by a human sponsor who presents you to the spirit, using their power as a kind of bridge (between the hands) to allow you to make contact with or see the spirit over their shoulder. In this model we can find a workable approach to the witches pact that strips it of its unnecessary Christian baggage.

What should go into the witch's pact? Well this could be as personal as wedding vows for a witch working alone. The pact may be simply between themselves and their fetch-mate, or it may specify the Master or the Queen of faerie, or other power spirit also. It is when working in covens that pacts truly come into their own, however. They can be viewed as the key to bringing together and reconciling a group of witches working with very disparate types of spirits. In which case the pact should include such things as a statement of loyalty to the coven's devil, as a way of uniting the practitioners, as well as certain agreed on matters of 'code' that will make sure that all the witches present are working toward the same common goals and keeping to certain rules that allow for healthy, safe and reciprocal interaction between the parties.

Wailing for the demon-lover

It is time, therefore, that you should apply for aid to such helpful Spirits. But will you have the strength of mind, the courage to endure the approach of Beings so different from mankind? I know that their coming produces certain inevitable effects, as internal tremors, the revulsion of the blood from its ordinary course; but I also know that these terrors, these revulsions, painful as they undoubtedly are, must appear as nothing compared with the mortal pain of separation from an object loved greatly and exclusively.
-William Beckford

Just as we discussed ways in which to guess the identity of the beast, we must also explore how one may discover if they have a fetch-mate or other human-like familiar and if not how one might attract such a familiar. Most witches I have known have already known they had a fetch-mate before they even knew what one was, but may have been at a loss as to how to reestablish contact lost in childhood or later. This is, of course, much easier than instructing someone on how to make themselves more likely to be chosen and so favoured by such a spirit.

If you are fortunate enough to have dreamed of your Other from an early age, or have other reason to know of their existence, stirring up that contact is likely to happen readily, assuming that true devotion to the goal exists. The first measure that one might take is to try to determine the spirit's nature. You may associate your early dreams or visitation with certain natural phenomenon. That phenomenon will be your immediate clue.

Did the spirit present surrounded by light? Do you associate them with air and wind and certain forms of weather? A season? Or do you associate them with heavier, earthier things? Do you think of them in relation instead to 'dark', mysterious and shadowy images, such as bones or certain animals or part animals? This can give you a hint as to whether your familiar is the 'faerie' type of being as appeared to faerie-doctors in the past and was generally more associated with light, music, bells, shining objects, beautiful singing and healing. Or whether the being is of a more chthonic type that might present itself in conjunction with the more traditional 'witches sabbat' environment. It must be said that infinite variations seem to exist between these two extremes, but having some idea if your familiar spirit reminds you of something you've read about in the testimonials will give you a better idea what sort of offerings and sacrifices to place for it.

As soon as you begin to have an idea what manner of being your fetch-mate is you should begin to make a space for them. This could be as primitive as an offering stone outside where you pour liquid offerings, or as ornate as an artwork with candles and incense and a complicated indoors shrine. Whichever you choose you need to begin to keep a schedule of offerings to them. You may like to use the traditional Western Occult system of planetary correspondences (please see appendix) to get an initial feeling for the nature of your spirit.

Sometimes you might find that the entity seems both Mercurial and Venusian, or Saturnian and Marsian together. Using this system can get you started on creating appropriate incense for the spirit, though it will naturally be replaced or refined as true communication opens up between you and the spirit. The more that you can find out about their nature the better you can tailor offerings to suit them. This is very important because there may be things that certain kinds of spirits find unsuitable. Throwing coins into wells for Underworld entities may be perfectly acceptable, and thus we can deduce that whilst the dead and many Underworld powers will accept money as a gift, there are types of fae beings that are offended by gifts of money. Whilst some spirits prefer milk as an offering others only want alcoholic spirits. If you cannot yet communicate directly with this spirit you may wish to use a form of divination as a temporary measure, such as a pendulum, or something else with yes/no options.

Once you have acquired the information to set up a shrine and a routine for honouring your spirit, you must be aware of the most important ingredient in successfully attracting the fetch-mate back into your life. This is: the power of your longing. The extent to which you want them is the power that your call-out will have. The fetch-mate will usually be attracted by the power of sexual longing as well as emotional longing. Fantasising about them and inducing orgasm has numerous uses. The first is through the passage of the breath, this we hear about in succubus and incubus lore. If one holds one's breath at the point of orgasm and draws the sexual power up to the head, breathing that power out in the direction of the fetch-mate is a very powerful drawing practice. Always let them know with some words or in your heart what your intention is and that you mean the power only for the 'true mate of your spirit.'

The other application for sexual energy is to become very aroused whilst fantasising about union with your spirit and then to fall asleep without reaching satiation. The power that is accumulated and unused here can often be used by the spirit to make initial contact in a lucid dream state. It should probably be mentioned at this point that you should only engage in such a practice if you are already confident with your other 'protections'. You should be certain of having at least one helper or guardian with you and have your working space well decked out in protective talismans that prevent the entry of destructive powers.

If you don't know whether or not you have a fetch-mate then it is probably best to ask to be shown the answer in a dream or divination. One can easily adapt traditional spells for seeing the identity of the future husband for this purpose and utilise certain nights of the year (like May Eve and All Hallows) that were believed to bring dreams of the future spouse. Girls have done many things from placing their shoes in the form of a T and leaving a silver penny in the moonlight near midsummer to dream of their future husband. Peeling an apple while sitting in front of a mirror at midnight is also a time honoured practice. But perhaps the most powerful is to take a spool of cotton out to the edge of a wild and waste place and throw the spool deeply into the trees. You should retract until the thread feels tight and close your eyes. Pray for your fetch-mate to answer you with a tug on the line if you have one. If the tug comes then one simply follows their thread out into the woods and is met by one's fetch-mate.

Of course there is also a history of explicitly trying to attract a 'daimon' for those who do not already have one. As far back as the *Greek Magical Papyrus* we find a spell to 'Acquire a Magical Assistant' (I give a modified version of this ritual later in the book.) WB Yeats, a noted occultist as well as poet, also wrote extensively on his attempts to 'acquire' a daimon.

The Suckling Imp

Eat me, drink me, love me.
  -Christina Rosetti, *The Goblin Market*

During the witch hunts it was believed that witches suckled imps from a hidden nipple on their body. Searching for this hidden nipple that the witch used to suckle the Devil or imps, involved stripping and shaving the accused, sometimes in semi public situations. The nipple was then searched for, often in the more 'secret' parts of the body. It is clear that a dimension of sexual intimidation was involved in this behaviour, making the accused feel increasingly vulnerable and breaking down their 'social self' so as to make them more pliable during interrogation. As a result the 'witch teat' concept tends to be approached with caution as likely an invention of the witch hunters. It seems likely that this mythos developed during the persecutions but it can also be shown to draw on older material.

The associations between witches and atypical lactation is unlikely to have been invented by the inquisitors. For a start this tradition seems to have been most popular in Great Britain and in American witchcraft, with its large population of British immigrants. These peculiarities, when aligned with the large amount of focus on imps in British witchcraft points towards there being something more behind the idea. Usually when an idea was drawn solely from demonological textbooks it tended to be generic across Europe.

'Witch milk' was a term for the milk that sometimes begins to be lactated by newborn infants due to hormonal disturbances in the body of the mother that they were exposed to in utero. It seems that superstitions regarding this 'witches milk' in babies is connected to the belief that witches themselves lactate a hidden milk for their imps or for the Devil. The anthropologist Herman Ploss states that in Germany, and also in England and Naples, midwives and grandmothers were convinced that if witch milk was not frequently and thoroughly expressed from the baby's mammary glands, it would be stolen by witches and goblins. Whilst the idea that *witches* suckled imps on a hidden teat was specific to certain areas, this belief seems to have been more wide spread. It was also accompanied by enough ritualistic behaviour and folk magic to make it unlikely that these beliefs were invented as late as the witch hunts.

In Germany it was believed that evil spirits, goblins, or imps cast the evil eye on babies in order to induce the formation of *Hexenmilch* (witch milk) and thus provide themselves with a source of nourishment. This superstition is confirmed by the fact that in Switzerland the appearance of lactation in a baby would evoke the statement (translated): 'He has an imp'. This milk had to be sucked out, and a knife with the edge uppermost was laid in the cradle.[25] Presumably the knife was expected to repel the imp. The Westphalian remedy was to make a poppet, resembling the bewitched infant, from rags and straw and then either to place the poppet in the baby's cradle or to nail the caricature over the door of the room.'[26]

So it seems that the tradition of striges, goblins or imps suckling humans for milk was widespread, the part that is more specific to Great Britain is the idea of grown adults having a hidden teat via which the imp is suckled. We cannot ignore the convenience of inquisitors having an excuse to strip search and humiliate the accused but the notion itself, of imps requiring some sort of nourishment from humans is certainly an older concept.

The earlier recorded forms of payment seem to have been blood sacrifice 'a chicken' or in the case of the Chelmsford witch Elizabeth Frances (1566) 'that every time that he did anything for her, she said that he required a drop of blood, which she gave him by pricking herself, sometime in one place and then in another, and where she pricked herself there remained a red spot, which was still to be seen.'[27] It seems that this 'red spot' left behind by the pricking for blood to give the imp or familiar might have preceded the witch's teat as the 'mark' to be searched for by the inquisitors.

If we delve into sorcery and shamanic practices in other nations we will quickly see that the notion of exchange between the human practitioner and the spirit is widespread if not, in fact, universal. Animal sacrifice has usually formed the 'staple' offering of vital forces in traditions as wide ranging as Siberian Shamanism and Haitian Vodou.

Even *The Secret Commonwealth* informs us that faeries covet a particular type of vitality unique to humans (or more correctly to living things.) So what we come to see through exploring the motif of the suckling imp is a better understanding of the economy of personal power that exists between a witch and a familiar spirit. And, as most no longer sacrifice live animals, it will usually be not just offerings of milk and food that we will exchange with the spirits we work with, but our own vitality, whether in the form of blood or sexual power.

In Aboriginal society this 'vital power' was known as 'fat', which makes sense when you consider the term 'fat of the land'. Witch-doctors were known for stealing 'fat' from other people in neighbouring communities much in the way witches were renown in Europe for skimming the cream or the fatty essence off the milk and stealing the 'vital essence' from crops. The image of fat makes a lot of sense when you consider that it is flammable. If you consider fire as the metaphor for the spiritual spark it requires fat to burn and it hungrily consumes it. In this way the fire of your spiritual work will consume the vital forces in your body and you must therefore be very vigilant about this and maintain your health.

As we have seen with larger powers like the *Leannan Sidhe*, the vital force required from the poet in return for her fire of inspiration can be so great as to cause early death. But the output in exchange with a smaller power, such as those that were referred to as imps or puckerils, that we have been calling fetch-beasts, is less onerous. Every interaction is built on fair exchange. So if one is hoping to experience the workings of a very powerful spirit one must be ready to make the necessarily sacrifices. A failure to understand this economy of power exchange between witch and familiar spirit is part of the reason so many fall by the wayside to madness, illness or early death upon this path. Our ancestors who were working within traditions with a certain degree of continuity (at least enough that one might have received superstitions about feeding imps) things were a little more straightforward.

Today most of us must strike up these deals with spirits on our own and many of us do a poor job at maintaining ourselves. In our eagerness to touch the divine and make contact with the world beyond the hedge we often allow ourselves to become a feast for spirits more powerful or more numerous than we can really support and end up dried up or cracked, like a leather cauldron exposed to fire with no water in it. It is the 'moisture' of the fat or vital force that stops the vessel going up in flames when the divine fire touches it.

When one no longer has the vital force to reciprocate with those powers, when one forgets that the body is the alembic of transformation, the temple in which human and daimon meet, as well as the sacrificial pit and the sacrificial flame, and does not treat it as such, it is seldom long before the body and fleshly brain are no longer able to sustain the touch of the fire.

Hedge-Crossing

I can imagine myself on my death-bed, spent utterly with lust to touch the next world, like a boy asking for his first kiss from a woman.
-Aleister Crowley

Every true witch is born with an unquenchable thirst to touch what is beyond, to break through to the Other that lies beyond the boundary markers, to go outside the mind-parameters of the 'town' and out into the wild beyond. For most of us such a state is not really very far away, it is the underside of our own nature. But undoubtedly most of us have developed numerous defences that keep those influences out. For when we are ignorant of them and not equal to the task of riding the wild beasts that dwell there, it is wise indeed to build good fences.

But for someone who has prerequisite nature and longing to cross the hedge the first thing that one needs to do is to stop thinking of this state as something that is acquired in a sudden flash. For many people there is a blurry state between visionary experience and normal consciousness that might seem a bit like visualisation. We need to allow this state again. Most of us knew how to do this as children, and it is probably experiences from this time that have led most of us to believe that we might be 'witches', but have had great walls built around our adult minds. As we discussed with dreams, we need to begin by making a conscious effort to cease categorising 'visualisation' and 'vision' as two hard and fast categories. Instead try seeing what you view in your mind as being steps of a ladder, with a deeper state of vision building with each step.

Begin your attempt to cross the hedge by focusing on your second skin. All witches have the ability to expel or create a kind of 'second skin', either in the form of a Double or an animal. This more subtle aspect of the physical body needs to be 'fed' and invigorated for a successful extension of consciousness, or 'flight' to occur. You can begin to become aware of the second skin via feeling for the tingling sensation of power when you lie very still and pay close attention to your sensory awareness. You may feel it well up to become something that explicitly wishes to escape through your mouth or chest or you may simply have to 'build' an image of your Double based around the tingling feeling of power in your body.

To enliven a Double bring together all of the urges and longings, desires and excess energy that you have in your body and consciously feed it into that tingling feeling. By doing this you are focusing your longing on crossing the hedge and feeding power into your second skin. This should cause a shimmering sensation in your body and around your forehead. You might find yourself aware of the beast-body and it stirring in your chest or lower, or even trying to get out your mouth, and this may feel like a great pressure that threatens to lift you bodily off the bed.

Envision then that you are pulling away from your body like

a sticky mist. Don't worry about it being 'real' just see and feel that desire and longing as a tangible 'thing' that's going to look around itself a bit. When this practice is done correctly 'visualisation' will naturally give way to 'vision'. This transition will happen only when you've fed enough vital force into the second skin. You should then be capable both of pulling free and transferring your conscious awareness to the second skin. Take some time to observe your everyday body from the perspective of your second skin.

Don't worry at first if you feel your consciousness to be somewhat divided between the two Skins. This is natural at first and will fade away as you become used to using your second skin. Generally speaking the longer the trance lasts for the deeper it becomes and the less the awareness of the everyday body.

Once you feel confident moving in your second skin allow yourself to wander towards a place where you feel an Otherworldly entrance might exist. During this period the trance state will usually be light to moderate. But when you try to make an assay through a door or over a hedge this is when you need to prepare for things to ramp up a notch. Remind yourself that your Double performs this activity regularly even when you don't know it, it ranges far beyond the body and is connected with everything it moves through. So all you are really doing is attempting to 'wake up' to this activity and claim possession of it. Your Otherworldly life has never stopped, simply because you stopped being aware of it. Continue down whatever path presents itself to you and whilst you are doing it relax your logical mind as much as possible. Afterwards is the time for analysing at what point a deep vision kicked in or at what point other entities entered and you were no longer 'visualising', not while you are doing it.

It may also help you if you walk on foot, whilst awake, down the path you mean to take in your Double, to the physical site of the Otherworld opening. You can even place markers such as coloured stones, or stones with special symbols on them that you remember to move from one to the other in your second skin. This can create a potent trance state in itself as you follow the stones as you did in your outer body. This way you have already programmed your Double with the path it must walk.

Some people also find being accompanied (or accompanying themselves) by a repetitive drumbeat or rattle to be helpful. The way that you cross the hedge will in essence depend on what powers reach out to you. One witch might experience their first deep trance where they meet familiar powers after ingesting mushrooms and be told that that is their method for doing their work. Another might be told that they are to sing particular songs over and over while rocking back and forth on the spot until visions begin to appear. Yet another may go out in a deep lucid dream, and have no other method of reaching that state.

Each of us must discover our own method and be gifted with knowledge of appropriate equipment and timing. If one is particularly stuck on this front a form of divination can be undertaken. The postulant should stand in a circle blindfolded while a helper has arranged different tools around the circle, a drum, rattle, a blindfold, something symbolic of dance, something symbolic of song, something symbolic of dreaming, and even some magical plants used for trance. The person should be spun around until dizzy and then allowed to grope forward until they inadvertently touch one of the tools. This method can be used where a beginner is simply not sure what method of hedge-crossing is best suited to them.

Of course not all people who 'cross the hedge' get any choice in the matter. Both faerie folklore from the past and modern 'alien abductions' detail humans being taken without their consent, changed and augmented in certain ways that might facilitate them being able to perceive faeries in the future, or developing other intuitive skills. These often-traumatic experiences have much in common with shamanic initiation stories from early in the shaman's career, where the shaman is often changed and reshaped for their vocation. These motifs still occur in transcripts from modern witches:

When I was about seven I had a dream that sinister faeries were gathered around the foot of my bed and they pricked the soles of my feet with a needle that injected something into me, which I felt spread through my body and I felt as if it was killing me. It was in that same year that I first began to have dreams which predicted small events and happenings, which continued and became much more intense when I grew up. I know when I was very young I 'flew' a few times in dreams that didn't feel like dreams over our local landscape but it is a far distant memory now, except that I remember the feeling was ecstatic and almost sexual even though I was so young.

Another witch who dreamed of being taken to cottage by a 'witch' and shown things experienced: '...nightmares about people cutting me in my sleep but no one believed me.' In many shamanic cultures traumatic experiences of cutting, piercing, dismembering, probing, heating and shaping were involved in the early hedge-crossing experiences. These things remind us that it isn't just us that enters the Otherworld, but the Otherworld entering and rearranging us.

Here Be Dragons

*The mystery religions were instituted in order to protect the
marvels of the commonplace from those who would devalue them.*
   -Peter Redgrove

One of the biggest boons that a witch can work to develop, when
it comes to hedge- crossing, is a good relationship with a
powerful site where crossing is easy. Every place has the capacity
to be a location for passage between the worlds, as the
Otherworld (as Other as it might seem to us) is always part of
everything we see and experience, we just fail to recognise it. So
the reason that some places make better crossing sites than
others might at first seem mysterious.

   In Alice Springs I was privileged to meet an Aboriginal
medicine man (nungkari). He described to me the way that a site
was 'active' in that a relationship exists between site, humans
and spirits, a three-way synergy that results in that place being

'sacred' or being a 'dreaming site.' The interaction between humans and spirits and site usually happens through the medium of story or myth. Key narratives are manifest at that place in certain ways that allow certain people that partake of those stories and/or a certain heritage to 'use' that site. A site can easily be useful in regards to experiencing spirit or *useless* to someone who does not share the right stories.

The narrative or 'deep myth' is a form of meeting place between spirits and man. We find that the power a particular site has as a crossing point doesn't just exist in the site alone (though power is certainly stronger in some places than others, it doesn't necessarily mean we can get good access to the Otherworld there) but in the relationship between myth, people and spirits connected with the site. That three ways crossroad can give a person a sort of 'leg up' when it comes to leaping the hedge. If you are not already aware of living near an active site that you have some chance of connecting with the deep, mythic dimension of, you might want to begin some investigation into finding one.

If you are fortunate you will already know of a place near you that has either a story or some superstition attached to it. Like the myth of witchcraft itself, most of these stories will be fragmented and usually it is only with the cooperation of the guardians of the site that the old synergy between person/story/land guardians ever becomes fully functional again. This is important because we come to the winding path of this particular narrative (this book) with a burning question. When we read about witchcraft in the past we want to know how we can enter into the fullness of those experiences that people seem to have integrated into their psyches so effortlessly in the past. This three-way story/person/land guardian synergy is one of the missing keys to this seeming disintegration of vision.

Many people think of 'The Sight' as a purely static thing that you either have or you don't. Even those who realise that you can develop these 'witch senses' don't realise the relationship that location-synergy has on Sight. Being able to cross the hedge is the fullest potential of The Sight, and having The Sight on a daily basis is just the ability to walk about with one foot on either side of the hedge. In some power locations otherwise 'non- Sighted' people can see incredible things, things so seemingly manifest that they take them for living people and animals.

The relationship between 'Sight and site' is another clue as to why so many people in pre-industrial times seem to have experienced vision not only so easily, but so intensely that they would say they went 'in their body' or that so and so appeared 'in the flesh.' When a person is deeply imbedded in a power site the veil between the worlds becomes very thin indeed. So if we wish to recapture some of what we have lost recreating these connections with place are of crucial importance. And the importance is not just in finding a long-standing power place, but in the building up of relationship. It may even be that the fact we think of some places as 'power places' is a vestigial remain of long standing power connections between humans and guardians of that site that still remain active. It is therefore possible that a 'power site' is simply a power site for humans, perhaps to certain non-human Others there is no such thing as a 'non power site' – and the implications of this are that with enough attention, cooperation from the guardians and time any site could (to some extent) become such a location.

Folklore provides us with a name for such a place, where access to the Underworld was very easy. In early-modern Wales these entrances to the Underworld, when they occurred in water were called a 'winch.' It was believed that deep lakes, pools, or sections of the ocean that contained a 'winch' could suck you down and you would be pulled into the winch and never seen again. This is probably a memory of an older understanding of the drawing power that such places have, and how if you encounter one it can literally seem like you have been pulled into the orbit of an experience rather than 'tried to jump the hedge.'

Locations like this can be found through dowsing or the use of a pendulum. Sites with a strong 'Underworld drag' will cause the pendulum to spin widdershins very energetically.

But it is also possible to predict their locations after looking at the land geomantically and considering the major sites and oldest tracks and how they connect together.

Once you find a place that you think has power, attempt an initial offering at the site. Make it known to the spirits of the site that you wish to start up an active relationship with them. If omens and dreams following the initial offering are favourable you might proceed to make regular offerings at this place. The better working relationship you build up first the more likely you are to have success when you try to use that site.

If you try to pass through and feel as though something invisible is pushing you back or anything menaces you, return home immediately.

In British folklore sites of sacred import such as holy wells, were all believed to be guarded by serpent or dragon spirits. These entities are the embodiment of the moving power in the land; its nerve, vein and vital network and unless they are well disposed to you, you will not be allowed to use the doorways that they guard. But if they decide to admit you as a part of themselves (often expressed initially by swallowing and regurgitating you), allow you to enter their power nexus, you will find that the fiery Sight that you are capable of suddenly jumps up a notch. But beware, not all of these guardians are initially disposed to be friendly to humans.

The Other Self

I equals not-I equals Thou
  -Novalis

When we begin to open our eyes to the older way of seeing, one of the first things that becomes apparent is how complex the 'self' is. Christianity has taught us to think in terms of 'body and soul' and yet to our pre-industrial ancestors, many of who though nominally Christian still thought in the older way, there were numerous dimensions to the 'self.'

When Claude Lecouteux looked at the notion of the 'free soul' in medieval and early modern Europe, he didn't just find that people could leave their body as an animal or were watched over by a 'fetch-bride', but also that people could 'Double' themselves, that is, produce a subtler version of their own shape. This 'other self' is the self that would journey to the sabbat or meet under the Downie Hills with the people of faerie. This humanoid double of the physical body seems to have been endowed with information and wisdom that the everyday self did not have, for it is credited with warning of the person's impending death.

The fact that the witch or faerie-doctor or werewolf possessed an 'other self' is the very reason for their power and their changed status both amid the human community and among the host of the dead or people of faerie. The werewolf had a part animal-part-human other self that gave the man certain powers that in his daily, normal human self he didn't possess. It is for this reason also that the witch could be considered 'one of the dead.' Because the witches' 'other self' acted as part of the company of the dead, and partook of their knowledge. It is also for this reason also that the faerie-doctor was not just considered a faerie-doctor but a faerie, or *donas de fuera*.

To draw together this Thread of older thinking with current occult teachings we might equate this 'other self' with the 'higher self', daimonic self, or genius, that in some forms of occultism the operator seeks to achieve union or knowledge of. It is possible here to experience some confusion between the other self and the fetch-mate, as both could be considered 'daimons' or 'geniuses' in the old sense of these words.

I think the easiest way to understand the difference is to point out that in Roman pagan thinking all things had their own 'geni' and every person possessed their 'genius.' To some extent this same thinking can be found among the Greeks in relation to the daimon. The sages understood every person to possess both an eidolon and a daimonic self. For the uninitiated the 'eidolon' (much like what is today called an ego) is all they know and the daimon appears as an external agency. But the goal of initiation is to unite daimon and eidolon into a 'whole self.' In the language of this book so far we could equate the eidolon with what we have been calling 'the Shadow' – this is the normal everyday consciousness of the person. The 'Skins' are other forms that may be animated by the Shadow, but the daimonic aspect of consciousness is the most mysterious of all, subtly working through the Shadow at all times, a direct spark of divine fire, the 'godhead' dimension of the self that few ever become aware of.

Whilst a daimonic self might be ascribed to every human, some experiencing it only as a 'guardian angel' and others coming to own it as themselves in higher form, the original pagan world was more complex than much modern occultism seeks to make it. Not everything that appeared to a human and was 'daimonic' (between human and godly) was therefore a manifestation of the higher or daimonic self. For instance the muses were their own individual entities and yet they inspired humans. The best way to understand the other self in witchcraft and the fetch-mate is to say that the other self is like a personal genius or daimon, but the fetch-bride, if one has one, is like a muse.

The worst thing we can do if we really wish to understand the Otherworld is to oversimplify what we see. There is a tendency toward classification, to ascribe one fetch beast and one fetch mate to all witches, or for other occultists to claim that all these things are simply aspects of the 'higher self'. Our ancestors did not see things this way. There is plenty of evidence of the subtle differences if we so much as look at two examples. One is of a Goldi shaman (shaman of the Amur Basin in Siberia) who told ethnologist L. Sternberg how he became a shaman:

One day, I was sleeping on my bed of suffering when a spirit approached me. She was very beautiful... She told me "I am the protector spirit of your ancestors, the shamans. I taught them how to shamanize; now I will teach you too." Then she added: "I love you. You will be my husband, for I do not have one now, and I will be your wife. I will give you spirits who will help you in the art of healing. I will teach you this art and I will assist you myself... If you do not do want to obey me, to bad for you! I will kill you." Since then she has never stopped coming to my house. I lie with her as if she were my real wife, but we have no children. She lives completely alone, without relatives in a little hut on the mountain. But she often changes where she lives. Sometimes she appears as an old woman or a wolf; that way people cannot look at her without being terrified.

Although this example is from a Goldi shaman rather than a witch it bears a great deal of similarities with witch testimonies like that of Andro Man who became the lover of the local faerie Queen, who even bore his children. It is clear that both these female spirits are not limited to the shaman or witch that they visit. The Goldi shaman's fetch-bride, as we would call it, makes it clear that she worked with his fore-parents before him, that he has in fact inherited her. Thus we can see, that like a muse, this entity does not come into existence purely for that practitioner and is not simply a manifestation of that person's 'higher self.'

In the world of witchcraft the Double can sometimes be the Shadow (everyday consciousness) inhabiting the second skin but at other times it is fully animated by the daimonic self, as can be seen in the following evidence:

The woman did what she said she would do, and around the middle of the night she saw a small, old neighbourhood woman riding a wolf and then saw her enter through the closed door. As the old woman approached the cradle the mother put the burning iron on her face and the woman left with a great cry. The next morning the mother went to the old woman's house, accompanied by some of the neighbours. They forced the gate and arrested the woman with the burned cheek.[78]

What is interesting about this testimony is that whilst the burn on the cheek proved the connection with the woman, the woman herself was confused and had no such memory of carrying out this 'other function' in her sleep. Stories of this kind are repeated over and over again with injuries being done to the Double appearing on the body of the person, but the level of power of the witch in question will determine whether there is *actual memory* of what they have done whilst out of their body. Whilst this seemingly daimonic dimension to the self that is not accessed by ordinary consciousness may certainly seem 'other' to someone who is unfamiliar with that part of themselves, it is not 'other' in quite the same way as the fetch-mate. The Goldi shaman's 'fetch bride' is actually able to say 'I will kill you!' and Isobel Gowdie's devil is known to hit her with a whip when she disobeys, all of which suggests the action of an at least partially independent entity with its own will.

All of this will sit badly for many immersed in mainstream Western Occultism, who will wish to see the daimonic self as the 'higher self' whose elevated nature is, of course, shown by it being without form or substance. Therefore it could not be injured while inhabiting a Skin or cause injury to the human self.

This kind of thinking about things being without substance is all part of the way that Christian thinking, and the many aspects of Neo-Platonism that resemble it in so many ways, has infiltrated to the core of most Western Occultism. Being between human and divine means being disembodied, not even possessing a subtle body and being a 'higher being' also apparently means being infinitely benevolent and not threatening to kill the person you work with!

These ideals about the nature of the divine were no part of the vision shared between shamanic cultures and the elder witchery of Europe. The spirits in their world were like forces of nature, in fact they may well have literally been forces of nature, whereas the spirits as we've come to understand them through the lens of Christianity and other flesh-hating ideologies have become this intellectualised concept of 'purity' and total benevolence.

If we are going to get closer to experiencing the daimonic dimension to the self, maybe even partially or wholly merging with that self in flight and perhaps interacting with spirit lovers, ancestors and/or animals, we will need to reconnect with the older sense of what these spirits are. They are something less like your guardian angel and something much more diverse and complex.

They might be like snow fall, like sunshine after rain, like a hurricane, like scorched earth, like a tempest at sea, like the silent depths of the sea, like a flock of birds taking to the sky. Or they might combine far too many of these natural powers to be easily understood by you. But the daimonic self is something you already know you are or want to be, because it is simply the 'over the hedge' part of yourself.

This is a great secret to the full realisation of hedge-crossing, it is no more or less than *being* that Other, or more properly merging that daimonic Other with the second skin. And the differing degrees of 'depth' of trance experienced are simply the different degrees to which you are fully merged, Skin to daimonic self and daimonic self to land spirit. When you are able to see through the eyes of the Other, the you that is immortal and in possession of far ranging knowledge and skills, your idea of what trance can become will open out new layers of profundity.

Here in the realms of recognising the face of the daimonic self we begin to look at how to go deeper into an Otherworldly state. When we go forth from our body we send our second skin, which we manipulate with the Shadow, also sometimes described as 'breath'. The next stage in opening up the greater potentials of trance, is to unite that second skin with not just this Shadow, but the daimonic self. There is a technique, adapted from one used by W.B Yeats, the renown poet and occultist, in the appendix of this book that aims at just this called 'Donning the Mask.'

Drenching the Ghosts

I am a child of the poisonous wind that copulated with the East
River on an oil-slick, garbage infested midnight. I turn about on my
own parentage. I inoculate against those very biles that brought me
to light. I am a serum born of venoms. I am the antibody of all Time.
I am the Cure.
-Ray Bradley

The *táltos* of Hungary were driven by a voracious appetite, as
though a spiritual fire that burned inside them drove them to
consume unusual amounts of fuel for their physical size. Within
the hunger of the *táltos* we can discern and uncover a mystery.
When sacrifice was performed in Hungary during the ceremony
of 'Drenching the Ghosts', the human *táltos* would be given milk,
mixed with the blood of the sacrificed animal, or simply drink
the blood of the sacrificial animal, which was literally believed to
'drench' the ghosts through the conduit of the sorcerer's body.

What is important here is that this reminds us that a human who straddled the hedge was not only themselves, but also the things that worked through them. Hungry ghosts could eat through the vehicle of a human being. And this tradition existed in Britain also with the notion of the 'co-eater' where a person could eat and eat and never be satiated. Often this is connected with changeling lore. Some changelings were believed to be unsatisfiable.

Recent archaeological evidence has shown that both in Ireland and Italy traditions relating to vampirism began at a much earlier time than was previously thought. Early medieval burials have been found in both countries, where a rock was wedged into the mouth of the dead to prevent them returning to feed on the living.

The dead appear in the folklore of the past as the ultimate site of ambiguity. They could bring blessings to the community if they were fed and revered, but if they were not they could turn hungry and angry and seek to predate on the very community that should have honoured them.

The witches that represent and actually embody those forces in their own flesh were therefore just the same. That sorcerer who was once a figure of ambiguity, associated with the dead and 'fed' in their place becomes a predator in the minds of a society that no longer fed the dead. It is possible that these witches did not just 'seem' this way to a culture that had rejected the Underworld as Hell and no longer felt that any good spirit returned to the world of the living, but it may have in fact created angry vengeful dead, and along with them *'malandanti'* witches who represented their now more vigorous taking force.

Even today when there is no longer a witch-hunt afoot or such vigorous propaganda to suggest that witches do maleficium I have collected at least one testimonial to suggest the presence of spontaneous maleficium. The individual concerned has many 'marks' to link her with the 'things in reverse' world of the dead, such as infertility and a physical asymmetry.

> *During my childhood there were several occasions where death seemed to follow my thoughts. These thoughts I would 'rock' to, sinking into trance -even as a five-year old-, with very deliberate and deathly intentions, casting ill-wishes to those who had vexed me. Filled with secrecy, I convinced myself over time that these happenings were far from maleficium and that instead I was just 'feeling' what was fated to happen, being filled with a 'seeing' of what was to come.*
> -Modern witch

The witch in question also experiences a strong relationship with the dead, and is frequently aware of them wanting something from her. If we understand the spiritual dynamic behind the traditions of 'drenching the ghosts' it can help us to better manage power exchange and also to understand why these eruptions of harm-doing have become such a large part of the witchcraft legacy. Harm doing is always existent in the natural world, but under conditions where 'take' has come to outweigh 'give' one could expect the denizens of the Underworld to be extra hungry and angry. And the necromantic witch, who is called to a relationship with the dead, may find themselves driven to act out those wishes and on a life-long quest to understand or control their own spiritual malevolence.

Coming to witchcraft from a modern post-industrial and post-scientific angle we are usually doomed to seeing a person as a discreet individual with a wall around their psyche. They are themselves and what is outside is 'Other.' But our ancestors did not see it quite this way.

Some witches had the hungry dead working through them, causing them to skim off the fat from the milk and spoil harvests. The *táltos* had all manner of hungry spirits working through them burning up all the 'fat' or vital force that they could get, and faerie beings at times could work in the same way when they granted inspiration.

This lore teaches us to better understand the power ecology that we are all a part of. If we are going to reactivate the spiritual streams of these old practices we are going to need to start acknowledging that people aren't just people and that we are not just 'us', but a site where certain things are occurring. You may well find that you need to take offerings on behalf of your spirits. This of course should never be used as an excuse for whimsically following cravings for things that are bad for you or others! One of the most important exercises of discipline that an occultist of any stamp should employ is making sure one never uses 'the will of the spirits' as an excuse to do something one simply wishes to do. Once you slide down that road it is often very hard to come back.

Keeping a clarity and purity of communication between yourself and the spirits will make it easier to know what they ask of you by way of offerings and how they wish you to take them, whether by swallowing them and using you as a conduit, or by simply pouring them on the ground. If you are scrupulous with this discipline from the first you will never have trouble knowing how and when to drench the ghosts.

Riding the Beast

The Way-farer in the Garden.... thus calls forth by his step the Wight of the Were, being the deific intersection of man and beast, standing between wild and tame. Where this path is walked in wisdom, knowledge... of fetch results; where it is trod by the fool abduction of mind and body results.
-Daniel Schulke

The first thing we need to understand about 'the beast' is that this power exists in everyone. Whether an animal familiar approaches you or not it is important to always remember that one still has an inner 'human beast.' When we seek to stir the shadows and awaken primal forces from their depths, as we do in witchcraft, we stir the beast. For most witches the inner beast will appear as a different species of animal. I have heard a few different connecting explanations for why the animal self of humans appears as other animals when we ourselves are already an animal. My favoured explanation is that as the species that the Master endowed with the cunning fire we are mercurial by nature and inherently our 'inner beast' has no one shape of its own but can assume the form instead of one of the 'ancestor animals.' The animal is not simply 'an animal' but the spirit of that beast as a whole, spirit of Wolf, spirit of Raven, spirit of Eagle.

Learning to properly harness the power of the beast is central to all successful witchcraft. The beast embodies our vitalistic forces and without this strong stimulation we would never have the 'fat' to burn a bright flame for long. So it could be said that the essence of success in witchcraft (that is, becoming power-filled without becoming mad and dysfunctional) is managing to raise the flame of the divine fire in balance with the vitalism of the beast. If one is too dominant over the other disaster will follow. Like any kind of 'riding' this is a precarious balancing act we engage in.

For some people 'riding' is how they will literally interact with the animal, as a mount that becomes partially an extension of themselves. For others they will transform into the beast, yet even then it is referred to as 'riding the beast', as opposed to being ridden by it, an occurrence which also sometimes happened but in certain circumstances only. Take for instance warrior cults where battle frenzy was sought via allowing the beast to temporarily dominate. Usually however one seeks to utilise the raw energy of the animal without being utilised *by it*.

All bestial species provide both blessings and challenges, with some, such as Wolf, providing very well known challenges. Werewolves for this reason were known to come in both benevolent and evil forms. By tapping this power you are awakening a primal energy in the self that like all primal powers is morally 'grey' in nature. It is up to how this power is channelled whether it becomes a useful force in the person's life or a dominant and destructive one.

The relationship of the fetch-animal form is normally a little different to that experienced in the case of were-creatures. The were-wolf, or in some cases were-fox or dog, (often found in the mazzeri) will experience transformation into this animal and usually no other, though like everything in the path of the Otherworld there are exceptions to this rule. The blending of that human being with the nature of that animal is very intimate and potent and it is not so much the familiar spirit that is that beast, but the witches themselves.

Often the were-creature will 'turn' periodically to carry out their Otherworldly work. This gives the individual access to a great deal of primal force that can be usefully deployed in sorcery that touches on very physical manifest matters like lust, primal life functions like birth and death, luck with money or locating lost objects. But the challenge for such a person is always to make sure that the fire of self awareness is kept high enough to balance the animal power. We have talked about the dangers of too much fire in relation to vital force, but we have not yet talked about the dangers of excess vital powers.

Excesses in these areas tend to lead to antisocial levels of lust and aggression untempered by softer feelings or self-control, objectivity or rationality, self-interest untempered by conscience or recognition of the fact that people are beings not objects, dominance seeking behaviour that is not tempered by proper respect for others and a very amoral type of animal cunning, and most of all by a pervasive state of 'unconsciousness' about oneself and one's own motives.

It is sad to say that witches of this sort are not uncommon, almost as common as the 'cracked vessel' type when it comes to 'high magic' practitioners. This is one of the dangers we court in stirring the shadows and making use of their primal vitalism. Alas without strongly cultivating these powers there is no way to safely encounter the fire. So as with riding any unruly creature we must rely on our sense of balance and human finesse. We must remember that as humans we are the artist and artisan species, capable of great subtlety and skill and it is this we must rely on when riding the beast, not brute force. Many animals have more brute strength or fierceness than us but no species is more subtle, more intelligent or cunning than man. The moment that we exercise brute force rather than skill on anything, we are as the term suggests, already being ridden by the beast rather than riding it and have lost before we even begun.

Riding Plants

As rank a witch as ever rode Ragwort
   -Traditional

Long before the image of the broomstick-riding witch became current in Britain, witches rode plants or animals. We have already talked at length about the occult significance of 'riding' animals. We have talked about how when we 'ride' something we partake of its power, are propelled by it but also in some way glide on top of it and direct its force. If we understand this fact the reason that witches 'ride' things will come to make more sense.

To animistic people it is not only animals that have a spirit but plants as well. So when we hear about witches riding the ragwort, fennel, sorghum or ointment lathed broomsticks, or the relationship between faerie-magicians and mushrooms, we will better understand what is occurring here. It is easy to understand how a witch might fly with the aid of a flying ointment because the ointments contained powerful narcotics and entheogens. What is not so often considered though, is the idea of non-entheogen plant helpers. The idea that the 'spirit of ragwort' or 'spirit of fennel' was a helper for these witches and this is why they 'rode' it, in a similar way that an aboriginal person might have 'honey ant dreaming' or know the spirit songs of a particular plant that they use for most of their healing work.

Fennel for instance is famed for its ability to hinder 'witches' from their will. As the *benandanti* men were inclined to dub the *malandanti* 'witches' we would therefore consider that the spirit of the fennel plant was an ally of the *benandanti* and other cunning folk who worked on counter magic, hex breaking and protection from maleficium.

Things that have this reputation usually have a correspondingly benevolent physical action. Sage, associated in many cultures with spiritual cleansing, is also an antiseptic, the same goes for salt. Garlic, which has such potent effects against vampires and all negative magic, also turns out to be one of the strongest anti-bacterial, anti-viral and anti-fungal plants. Similarly with fennel its actions in soothing the digestion, particularly in infants and increasing the lactation in nursing mothers, helps us to see why its spirit would be understood to be benevolent and productive.

Ragwort on the other hand is known as being a steed of witches, faeries and even the Devil, and has a stem that is poisonous to livestock. The plant is also incredibly invasive and grows in infertile soils where little else will thrive. It is easily possible to see how different types of witches might have formed allegiances with the spirits of these plants. Likewise sorghum, also known as 'broomcorn' is famous for its ergot outbreaks. Some species of sorghum also contain hydrogen cyanide in the early stages of their growth, in amounts lethal to grazing animals. Plants that are under stress can contain lethal does of cyanide even later in their growth. So Sorghum is both a food crop and a potentially deadly poison, you don't have to think too hard to imagine how a helper of this type could be relevant to the ambiguous dead and witches who work with them!

Many people who engage the spirit of witchcraft in modern times, trying to tap into traditional cunning arts, look to connect with a fetch-beast or animal formed familiar. But due partially to the modern drug culture, very few people are able to look at entheogens (I use this term rather than hallucinogens because it suggests their sacred function) in anything other than a materialist and consumerist manner. They look at the plants (marijuana or 'magic mushrooms') like a product that they can get some fun sensation out of. Instead, if one wishes to cultivate 'plant familiars' and learn to 'ride plants' it would be better to master the art of 'riding' those that don't have such potent inner fire, the non entheogens. The spirits of these plants are not so powerful and are less likely to end up riding you! And if you are going to use particular herbs in protective sorcery, or any other type of sorcery for that matter, it would pay (in the form of stronger outcomes) to become familiar with the 'non ordinary' dimension of that plant first.

When it comes to knowing one of the smaller plant spirits the first good step is to grow one. Although it is possible to commune with the spirit of a plant just from ingesting it or smoking it or even using it in sorcery, it is far more powerful if you can know that plant throughout its growth and harvest from it in a sacred manner. You will need to spend time with that plant in a semi-entranced state. Speak with it and let it know of your desire to work with it at a spiritual level, ask it to show you how it wishes to be seen. Often the active spirit of the plant will appear as a human or an animal. It may offer you prayers or songs that you can use to rouse it when you wish to harvest it, use it for medicine or charms. Anything it offers you by way of help should be greeted with offerings. It is best if you think of this plant as an embodied helper spirit. Anything you use it for will be doubly powerful on account of this.

When you have become proficient at this with at least one non-entheogen you might want to start getting to know a psychoactive plant at a spiritual level. Of course many of these plants are restricted by law (such as marijuana, *salvia divinorum*, peyote, and magic mushrooms among others) so it would be wise to look into what plants you may legally utilise in your state, for I would not want to suggest that someone break a law.

Having conducted research into legalities it is then necessary to either encounter the plant as a dried sample or seek it in the woodlands, as is the case with various species of mushrooms. The first thing you should remember if you intend to approach a plant that is an entheogen, and try to convince it to become your helper, is that you needn't consume it to begin working with it. Entheogens are not just 'little spirits' but whole and powerful teaching intelligences in their own right. They will teach you how to 'ride' them correctly, if you show them the proper respect. If you treat them in a consumerist manner they will simply consume you in return.

The first things you should seek to understand about any plant that you deal with is the nature of its power. Does this plant have a chthonic quality about it? Or is it associated with faeries of light or healing? Is its reputation sinister or holy? What does it smell like and what are its physical properties? These are the same questions we ask ourselves when dealing with the 'little spirits' of the plant kingdom. But we must ask them all over again when dealing with the great teaching intelligences, and we must be very careful. Because when you seek to achieve your trance via a power plant, you are in fact *riding the trance of that teaching intelligence,* rather than your 'own.' One must be fully aware of the 'leg up' they are receiving.

With something like a mushroom, whether it is the psilocybin mushroom or the *amanita muscaria,* you are clearly looking at a power that links one to the subterranean regions. Mushrooms by nature are an interconnected fungus that thrives in damp mossy environments among the forest leaf litter. Their power is therefore about connecting you with the physical web of living beings and helping you to descend into the Underworld and talk with the dead. But there are differences still between the red and white spotted amanita mushroom, and the gold topped psilocybin. The amanita's power is darker and earthier, whereas there is more 'fire' in the gold top. The gold top allows us access to the fire-within-the-earth, whilst still being very earthy, there is something very 'fae' about this mushroom. It has been my experience that they will only reveal themselves to the right person and can be missed in the forest by others. It is also important to note that if you are someone who springs, as I do, from a European ancestry it was most likely these two forms of mushrooms that were the entheogens used by our ancestors.

Other entheogens such as Marijuana (the holy status of this herb is immediately given away by it's name 'Lady Mari', which probably references the Basque goddess Mari, though its use is currently restricted in most countries) contain an extremely potent fiery nature. People who find they have helpers or an original self that appear to them with 'sky based imagery' will usually be the ones to find this herb the most potent helper, and yet at the same times these people are those most in danger from misuse of it.

Abuse of this helper plant is so wide spread in our culture that it can be difficult to establish sacred use of it in people who have come to see it as a source of recreation. If one does choose to try to learn to ride this plant they will need to be very careful that they do not burn themselves out. Regular breaks from it should be taken, especially in the early stages of walking our path. And I have encountered enough people who fail to take into account these warnings that I am hesitant to even recommend its use.

As far as entheogens go flying ointment is probably the best known of plant-based methods of achieving the witches' flight. Several recipes exist, all of which are extremely dangerous but likely to be effective in the right dose. They contain both hallucinogenic and narcotic ingredients, which means that awareness of the daily body is likely to be completely cancelled and the potency of Otherworldly flight therefore greatly enhanced. Obviously only a trained naturopath or medical herbalist would really be qualified to properly put one together.

Whether we choose to try to construct a safe flying ointment today we can certainly understand that deadly poisons like Belladonna and Aconite would bring people closer to the borders of the world of the dead. And it is known that these plants when used together link the witch directly to the experience of the Grand Sabbat and spirit flight. We also know, given the strong place of ointments in witchcraft, either applied directly to the body or on the riding pole or broom (going as far back as the account of witches in *The Golden Ass* nearly two thousand years ago) that riding plant helpers has always been an aspect of The Art.

When You Have to Come, You Will Come

Go by coombe, by candlelight,
by moonlight, starlight, stepping stone,
and step o'er bracken, branches, briars,
and go tonight, and go alone...
　　-Terri Windling

These days it is common to see modern paganism reproduce ancient festival dates in a sort of regular pattern throughout the year. This approach is not sufficient for the witch. A witch's inter-action with the tides of power must be directly linked to the movements of the unseen. Celebrations or special activities that occur throughout the year will be timed with a mind to this. For different types of witches and Otherworldly beings certain times may be found more important than others.

The full moon may take on special importance for some types of Witch more than others. As early as the 1500's there is evidence of an association of the moon at its height with wolf-turning. Whereas the 'fox turning people' of Wales were believed to go forth in fox-skin during the Winter and Summer Solstices particularly.

In folklore there are as many different 'important times' as there are types of ecstatic sorcerer. The *benandanti* ride on the Ember Days and have a special smaller meeting every Thursday. The Ember Days were roughly in line with the four major fire festivals celebrated by modern witches. These were times of prayer and fasting that probably helped people reach the required state of consciousness. It was considered important to have fresh water left out on the Ember Days in case any spirit-being returning from these events needed to quench their thirst or their horses.

The Eve of St John or Midsummer is given as the height of faerie activity, for this reason it would take on particular importance for 'faerie-seers' and anyone working with a faerie familiar. It is traditional to leave out strawberries and milk for them on this night. But it should also to be remembered that it was a dangerous time to be out and about where you were liable to become 'pixie led.' Twilight and early dawn are power times for faerie, and Midsummer in the northern hemisphere produced twilight like conditions almost all through the night at the height of midsummer.

The depths of winter are more associated with the Wild Hunt and the dead. At the beginning of winter the Shining Court (usually what is referred to when people talk about 'faerie familiars') yields to the Court of Winter. This involves Hell Hounds, wandering spectres and the presence of numerous more Underworldly beings including sometimes The Black Faced Huntsman himself (the King of the Underworld, whose black face connects him with Gwyn ap Nudd or Arawn of Welsh legend. The English legend of Herne the Hunter also associates this figure with having stag antlers upon his head.).

Most people consider the 'change over' of the courts to fall on Roodmass and Hallowmass respectively, though in some places it will be felt as early as the equinoxes. Hallowmass is when the dead return to the earth to be entertained, fed and reunited with the living.

Vampires and other malevolent types of witches who are compelled to 'feed' on living people to satiate the death-powers, were believed to undertake their flights during a blood moon (when the moon appears red during and eclipse or other climatic event.) Eclipses of any kind are times when maleficium is at its strongest. Some covens of witches also timed their monthly meetings via the fullness of the moon. And whilst the *benandanti* favoured Thursday for their meetings (betraying a Jupiterian current to their magic and association with protective warrior gods like Thor), Friday has always been associated with witch-craft. Thus a Friday that falls on the 'sinister' number thirteen also had traditional associations with witchcraft.

How a witch or coven today decides to feast and placate the dead, to interact with and offer to faerie, guarding against foreign vampiric intrusion, leaving offerings for the Host, and honour the change-over of the Courts will depend on many factors. First of those will be what powers are working through that witch or the witches in that coven. If one found themselves a modern-day *benandanti* for instance, he might desist from hanging up garlic and fennel to hinder witches from their will in a space that he might share with others whose powers might work differently! Just as a faerie-seer may wish other people to leave iron objects far away from the space they come together in. These sorts of peculiarities will effect how much attention is paid to different times of year as well.

The other necessary condition for establishing a living sorcery practice around the year's cycle is the land upon which you live. You must pay attention to the flux and flow of the powers around you on that space for some time before you will be able to truly respond to the times of power. Stationing feast days, maybe even fasting and prayer around the Ember Days, leaving out water for the Riders, offering to faerie at Midsummer and a large propitiation of the Dead at Hallowmass will certainly be on your agenda. But exactly how you place these days, exactly when you celebrate them should be a matter of your direct experience of the Otherworld, as it was for those who came before us.

We will not succeed in making Otherworldly tides dance around an eight-spoked wheel of the year, it is us that must do the dancing in response to the movements of greater powers. You will look for physical as well as Otherworldly signals. You will look for the first blossom on the hawthorn to declare it Roodmass but you will also become familiar with a special feeling, a taste or a smell in the air that heralds the approach of the Shining Court.

Likewise with the approach of winter you will note the mists in the morning and the days beginning to shorten, the leaves withering from the oak who is the strongest and whose leaves hang on till near the end. But you will also notice the thickening of the air with the presence of ghosts and a certain melancholy, as though the earth were breathing out the past.

A Tale Shared

We teach by poetic inference, by thinking along lines that belong to dreams and images.
-Robert Cochrane

Most people think that stories are something that happens inside books, and that narratives belong only to tales and epics. But if we come to see the world from the perspective of Fate we soon come to see that the world is comprised from a variety of competing narratives. Those who called themselves 'werewolves' had one particular narrative that they were following, one that was different to the story that the outside world had about them. When we deal with the records of witch-craft in Europe we are always dealing with this sense of competing narratives. We encounter numerous sub-narratives that different people had about certain ecstatic groups, we encounter somewhere behind it all a shadowy meta-narrative that binds together this world of spirit flight, hedge-straddling, skin-turning, animal riding and sabbat attendance and we encounter, written over the top, the story of the inquisitors and the mainstream Christian majority.

As people coming to the story of European Witchcraft much later in the tale, we find some parts of the narrative garbled, and other things appear clearer and more panoramic than ever. We talk about a 'story' rather than a tradition because we acknowledge that we are part of a grand narrative that is always spinning itself out and changing. Each fully realised Witch becomes a new, temporary organization of the story.

It is clear from reading the testimonies of modern ecstatics who have re-entered the story of Traditional Witchcraft that some of the smaller stories have merged into larger ones, things that were once distinct chapters have run into each other and become confused. And yet it is still recognisable as the same story being told.

A coven, or any other smaller grouping of witches, is formed up within the auspices of that story and yet each person who enters the story brings with them the potential to eventually change the tale in some way. It is fair to say that each person who enters always changes the story but as a student one attempts to disturb it as little as possible, because one seeks the sponsorship of that story.

Upon entering Traditional Witchcraft as currently manifest in the coven's story you get access to broader and older narratives that went into the weaving of it and you get to draw on their power. All stories are a form of power and whenever we enter into one, we do what is called 'suspending disbelief' and become emotionally involved with that reality, we allow ourselves to fall under the spell of something, but at the same time we receive power from it. Great sorcerers are usually master storytellers and weavers of these kinds of spells. And what we would call a 'fully realised' witch has become a new manifestation of the story they originally entered quite passively.

So as a student one enters the story of witchcraft and allows it to rewrite them, they enter its universe and allow themselves to function under its laws and its vision. And this conceals an important magical truth: he or she who wishes to be a great enchanter must possess the ability to be enchanted. Unless you are capable of falling under a spell, and later knowing that you are falling under a spell and allowing yourself to be ensorcelled and in fact becoming an active participator in this process, it is unlikely that you will have the sensitivity to beauty and the subtlety to ever weave spells for other people. This is a little like the way that someone who does not know how to love is unlikely ever to be loveable.

You must first fall in love with a pre-made story and enter into it on the story's own terms before you will gain the power to change the story through yourself. You may not think that you would ever want to change the story, or if you are a particularly dominating person you may feel quite the opposite and completely understand why someone would want to change the story. But I can say now that those with a strong capacity to love will have more luck.

Interestingly both giving yourself over to a story and the willingness, once it is fully understood and a part of you, to change it, are both manifestations of love. Because the fully realised witch changes the story from the right space, not to write her petty human ego over the top of something beautiful and divine in a kind of 'so and so was here' gesture, but because the very love they feel for the story makes them wish to involve themselves in it, blend with it, breed with it almost. Think of the desire a man may feel to impregnate a woman. If he wishes to impregnate her to make a third thing, so that he can blend with her and become a part of her then he is more likely to get further than if he wishes to do it to dominate and control her and make something in his own image only! A story is much like a woman in this sense. It is a mystery. It should be approached out of love. Seek to understand it, not to manipulate or control it in your own image. Seek to *know* it and you will find its gifts to be beyond price.

Here you begin your practice in 'being enchanted.' It sounds strange that we talk about 'being enchanted' as an active activity rather than something that is done to you. This is because as a Witch once you start opening your eyes and becoming increasingly aware of things that are usually unconscious, you begin to realise you are participating in many processes. You are a participator in the grand system of Fate and you are also a participator in your own enchantment. So when we really think about it, it will no longer seem strange to say that there is a skill to being enchanted, to being spellbound.

So far we have talked about The Sight and crossing the hedge in terms of a passive opening up, but there is more to the picture. The ability to allow something to enchant you happens in direct relation to how much love you have for something. This might seem like a simple key but it's a potent one. If you love the Master with a huge fire of devotion His ability to enchant you will be greater, because love is the other secret key to attainment, a key that belongs to Our Lady.

One of the best uses of one's time as a sorcerer, in addition to petitioning the Master to open your Sight, is to begin devotions to The Queen of faerie asking her to give you the gift of great passion. The Master gives us the key to the unseen door, but without the seal of heart-fire that the Lady grants us, the longing and the passion for the story, all our hopes will peter out.

As you set out further into your journey deeper into our story remind yourself of the value of enchantment. Learning how to become enchanted is the beginning of learning how to enchant. But enchantment is frightening. Letting go of oneself enough to enter into a story that you don't fully as yet understand, to agree to work along its plot and come to its conclusions requires both bravery and subtlety but most of all it requires love. I have heard it said that subtlety and cunning are the gift of the Master, love and passion are the gift of the Lady and courage is the gift you give yourself as a representative of mankind and mankind's dignity. And I think these are wise words to keep in mind as one takes one's first step into the world of Stories.

Our faerie tale is something you can only reach by going down the rabbit hole, so begin to exercise your ability to be enchanted. Stop and find something beautiful and gather yourself into the moment. By this I mean a state where you are not thinking about the past or the future, just be completely in the presence of that beautiful thing. Try and find something that if you look at it or listen to it long enough it can make you cry. It doesn't matter what it is or how long it takes you of meditating on its beauty to get this response, but a good sorcerer must be able to conjure-forth powerful emotions in themselves.

This state as well as one of seething, dirty malice must both be reachable for you and you need to be able to find keys that create these states in you. Do not think that you don't need to create the state of 'dirty seething malice' as you never intend to curse, instead think of it as exercising the full range of human emotional potential. Even if your purpose as a witch is to heal you must at least attempt to know the emotions that lay a curse down before you can lift one.

But in the beginning it is mainly the ability to be utterly enchanted with something that you will need. The rest of your 'range' can be worked on later. Once you have found one thing that creates this state in you try and broaden your repertoire. See how many types of enchantment you can make yourself subject to. Find things that create states of pure aesthetic bliss, things that make you shiver and feel uncomfortable, things that make you feel lustful. And then try things that make you feel odd combinations of feelings at the same time. This practice will sensitise you and increase your awareness of things, as well as make you more able to experience a state of enchantment in ritual.

It may well be asked why we need to do this kind of practice. If the spell of something is strong enough surely we shouldn't have too much trouble falling under it? There is actually a very good reason we are not more susceptible to them and to Otherworldly phenomenon in general, it is for our own protection. Our minds have evolved to bloke out this input for survival reasons. It is only when our helpers and ancestral protectors (if they are strong and we are fated to survive) are convinced we can integrate that material successfully that they will open those gates for us. The good news is that this kind of practice, everything that we have been doing in fact, stretches those muscles and makes it not just more likely to happen but more likely to happen with some level of safety.

If we work on learning to become enchanted when we so will to be we are not longer the victim of enchantments or able to be easily led astray by powers that do not wish us well. We are able to instead *choose* what spells we fall under.

Because the great and terrible truth about Stories is that we are all living in them already, the plots and characters have simply become so familiar and seem so inevitable to us that we can see no other way that our lives could go. This is how Fate operates, the 'doom' she has in store for us is written in such a story. She is the artist of artists. And yet the Master has won for us the potential to be lesser artists ourselves, to take some part, through him in rewriting the story that will define our lives. And witch-craft, at its core, is about seizing and embodying that artistry.

The Mystery of the Sabbat

Carouse ye with my Satyrs and embrace the Succubi raised from thy own Desires; swoon ye in rapture, in the nimbus of fever billowing over the lily-field of the Night.
  -Andrew Chumbley

In the story of witchcraft 'the sabbat' became something almost as broad as the word 'witchcraft' itself. Any kind of spiritual meeting, from a coming together of the *benandanti* for combat, to a gathering of humans and faeries, through to witches flying on broomsticks and feasting on unbaptised infants, all came to rest under the banner 'sabbat.'

As Eva Pocs points out, the main difference between so called faerie feasts and witch sabbats are the infernal images of darkness versus the sound of bells, beautiful music, light and shining things. Other than that the same things happened, food was consumed, there was a greater emphasis on music and dance in the faerie narrative but dance still occurs in the witchcraft sabbat, sex features in both narratives. Were they originally one thing? A meeting of powers that could be associated with both the dead and faerie? Or were they originally something different?

I would consider that when in doubt it is always better to assume and allow for more diversity rather than less. The Otherworld seems to be an infinitely diverse place that is seldom as simplistic as our human categories. So why must all faeries be the human dead? Could some consist of the human dead or even could they have some of the human dead among their number and yet be a different type of daimon? Could we allow for the idea that some forms of daimons were more associated with the sky and consciousness and others with material processes and the soil? If there are so many different types of witches why can't there be different types of gatherings? Perhaps different entities meet up in one Grand Sabbat? Let us look at a couple of sources to try to get a better understanding of this matter.

The following case of the 'Faerie Drummer Boy of Leith', told by George Douglas in his *Scottish Fairy and Folk Tales*, is a good example of a faerie gathering inside a hollow hill.

About fifteen years since, having business that detained me for some time at Leith, which is near Edinburgh, in the kingdom of Scotland, I often met some of my acquaintances at a certain house there, where we used to drink a glass of wine for our refection; the woman which kept the house was of honest reputation among the neighbours, which made me give the more attention to what she told me one day about a fairy boy (as they called him) who lived about that town. She had given me so strange an account of him, that I desired her that I might see him the first opportunity, which she promised; and not long after, passing that way, she told me there was the fairy boy, but a little before I came by; and, casting her eye into the street, said, 'Look, you, sir, yonder he is at play with those other boys,' and designing him to me, I went, and by smooth words, and a piece of money, got him to come into the house with me; where, in the presence of divers people, I demanded of him several astrological questions, which he answered with great subtlety ; and, through all his discourse, carried it with a cunning much above his years, which seemed not to exceed ten or eleven.

He seemed to make a motion like drumming upon the table with his fingers, upon which I asked him, whether he could beat a drum? To which he replied, Yes, sir, as well as any man in Scotland; for every Thursday night I beat all points to a sort of people that used to meet under yonder hill (pointing to the great hill between Edinburgh and Leith). How, boy? quoth I, What company have you, there? There are, sir (said he), a great company both of men and women, and they are entertained with many sorts of musick, besides my drum; they have, besides, plenty of variety of meats and wine, and many times we are carried into France or Holland in a night, and return again, and, whilst we are there, we enjoy all the pleasures the country doth afford. I demanded of him, how they got under that hill? To which he replied, that there were a great pair of gates that opened to them, though they were invisible to others; and that within there were brave large rooms, as well accommodated as most in Scotland.

Here we can see certain features: being carried long distances (something suggestive of flight) music, good food and wine and being invited into a hollow hill. Isobel Gowdie, who we know as famous for many workings of maleficium was also invited into and feasted inside the 'Downie Hills.' The main differences are that Isobel Gowdies' vision included the fighting of fierce animals, and 'elf-boys' that were whittling elf shot, which would later be used to kill humans. There is, on the other hand, nothing malevolent about the faerie-boy's narrative of the faerie meeting. In every other respect the two occurrences resemble each other.

This is not, of course, to say that the Shining Court are incapable of moments of malevolence, but merely to note that 'darker' imagery occurs in the typical 'witches sabbat' than at the faerie meeting, even though both at times will occur inside Hollow Hills. It is probably safe to say that there are many types and tribes of preternatural beings that may invite humans to meetings, and though we can use the term 'sabbat' to cover all of these occurrences we must be sensible to the fact that not every 'witch' is necessarily taken to the same type of meeting. The *benandanti* went to their own meetings and once a year went to a grand meeting where they also saw the *malandanti* whom they were accustomed to fight with, just as one example. There seem to be extremes of sabbat confessions that reflect a deeply 'infernal' feeling and 'fairy narratives' that describe just the opposite. As Eva Pocs puts it:

> *Witches with fairy attributes are mentioned several times in the trial records. They brought glittering beauty to the houses in which they appeared, and they abducted their victims into their companies and their fairy-like witches sabbats by making music and dancing. Negative witch characteristics are totally absent from some of these source narratives, which depict an alternative world full of beauty and joy that contrasts with the miseries of the material world.*[29]

The demonologists tended to resolve this problem by imposing the idea that both were the same thing, that these images of beauty were merely illusionary trappings that would soon fall away and show bones, raw meat, dung and dirt underneath. In this way the idea of any diversity in witch meetings was done away with. Despite this confounding of the two extremes of witch meetings with each other, it seems likely that the infernal model was also very ancient, and this fact may be as simple as the way most shamanic cultures see the Otherness in terms of 'Underworld', 'Upperworld' and 'Middleworld', with some possessing many more gradations within these categories.

In Ireland the following story was told about the origin of

faeries, that seems to point to just such an understanding, despite the Christian gloss over the top:

> The Sidhe, or spirit race, called also the Feadh-Ree, or fairies, are supposed to have been once angels in heaven, who were cast out by Divine command as a punishment for their inordinate pride. Some fell to earth, and dwelt there, long before man was created, as the first gods of the earth. Others fell into the sea, and they built themselves beautiful fairy palaces of crystal and pearl underneath the waves; but on moonlight nights they often come up on the land, riding their white horses, and they hold revels with their fairy kindred of the earth, who live in the clefts of the hills, and they dance together on the greensward under the ancient trees, and drink nectar from the cups of the flowers, which is the fairy wine. Other fairies, however, are demoniacal, and given to evil and malicious deeds; for when cast out of heaven they fell into hell, and there the Devil holds them under his rule, and sends them forth as he wills upon missions of evil to tempt the souls of men downward by the false glitter of sin and pleasure. These spirits dwell under the earth and impart their knowledge only to certain evil persons chosen of the Devil, who gives them power to make incantations, and brew love potions, and to work wicked spells, and they can assume different forms by their knowledge and use of certain magical herbs.
>
> The witch women who have been taught by them, and have thus become tools of the Evil One, are the terror of the neighbourhood; for they have all the power of the fairies and all the malice of the Devil, who reveals to them secrets of times and days, and secrets of herbs, and secrets of evil spells; and by the power of magic they can effect all their purposes, whether for good or ill. The fairies of the earth are small and beautiful. They passionately love music and dancing, and live luxuriously in their palaces under the hills and in the deep mountain caves; and they can obtain all things lovely for their fairy homes, merely by the strength of their magic power. They can also assume all forms...[30]

Of course, it is not often allowed to any of the faeries to be creatures of the air, because Heaven is 'up' in Christian thinking and if the faeries are fallen angels none of them can abide there. But it is noteworthy that they are still divided into those who live above the earth, below the waves and below the earth, with the last being explicitly associated with the doings of witches and the Devil. This seems to point to an older system of dividing faeries into different kinds, a system that might pre-date the idea of the 'dark sabbat going witch' and the 'faerie-doctor witch'. The evidence suggests that even in folklore, outside the minds of the interrogators, there are still a tribe of spirits that are more attuned to matters of darkness. Another folkloric testament gives it differently, making the parallel with the 'tiered reality' of shamanic thinking much more obvious again:

> My father's and grandfather's idea was that the fairies tumbled out of the battlements of heaven, falling earthward for three days and three nights as thick as hail, and that one third of them fell into the sea, one third on land, and one third remained in the air.'[31]

Here in this Manx version the ocean takes the place of that which is 'beneath.' In this version faeries of the air are allowed and we see the Celtic 'three realms of earth, ocean and air' concept.

As further evidence that the 'infernal extreme' isn't always the product of the minds of the interrogators I present a modern testimonial in this 'infernal' (by which I mean chthonic rather than 'evil' in the standard Christian sense), and in this case bestial, vein.

Modern Example:

> There were times of the year when I'm sure I partook in the Great Hunt. Where we travelled as a black snarling mass that rode through roads half familiar, some on horseback, some running, some as beasts, some not. It was chaotic and visceral and instinctual.

Sometimes the roads would converge and great bonfires of the hunted were herded up into them. At other crossroads were couples engaged in a variety of sex acts. And then, at other times in the year, the urge to travel as a dog would vanish, and I would doubt my sanity until the months rolled by and it would all begin again and I would be surprised that I ever doubted how real the experience was.

And in between these two extremes, one that is dark and instinctual and full of sex and violence and the other extreme where everything is full of beautiful music and dancing and light, there are also numerous gradations. It seems that when most people make it to a sabbat they find themselves at an event that contains some mixture of these characteristics, and we are not remiss in terming these events 'sabbats.'

Generally speaking it was the fetch-mate or other familiar spirit that conducted the soul of the witch to sabbat, at the appropriate hour. And we as modern witches must similarly rely on the auspices of our helpers. However, it is indicated in a few sources that the mere fact of saying, leading up to the date when the relevant event is set to occur (ember days, full moons, or other date important to one's nature) aloud three times that tonight you will go to the sabbat or answering your spirit 'yes' three times in response to such a question, will result in someone arriving to take you.

Shaped in the Forge

So shall he be accomplished in the furnace; so shall he see things that ought not to be seen, sights that are abominable, and secrets that are unutterable. So shall he read elder truths, sad truths, grand truths, fearful truths. So shall he rise again before he dies.
   -Thomas de Quincey

In most shamanic cultures being 'made' consists of an initial initiatory crisis, followed by some smaller 're-makings' that may be slightly less terrifying. In many of the shamanic cultures closest to Europe, such as the Siberian and Lapp shamanic traditions, this 'remaking' is seen as heating and shaping in a forge, with the figure of the smith having a power almost equal to that of the shaman. There is certainly some suggestion that this tradition extended into witchcraft, as there is a long tradition, particularly in Britain, between the Devil and Blacksmithing. Modern Traditional Witches have seized on this tradition with their large focus on the figures of Tubal Cain or Azazel, as the 'god of witches' who are both associated with smith craft.

Unlike shamans in other cultures witches today function without a fully weaved cultural structure around us to 'hold' us through this experience. Most of us are lucky to have so much as a mentor to discuss our work with and even that won't help you to get time off work for your initiatory crisis! For most of us it will be necessary to cultivate quite an intense understanding of it to try and prepare ourselves as best we may. We need to shine light into the dark on this topic, because otherwise we will have no framework to help us understand when that great and terrible challenge begins. We do not have records of the emotional adjustments that were experienced by witches in early modern Europe, but we can certainly draw on a large body of knowledge that has accumulated around today's witches, and how the process of 'being made' affects them.

At the beginning of your journey down the crooked road you will be gifted with power in various forms, some will be vital force and some will be fire. When you receive the full awakening of the beast you will receive more vital force. But fire may also be given to you either by a mentor passing you power, or by the insertion of power into the body by spirit beings, or even by being gifted with new spiritual tools in the Otherworld.

It should be noted here that the process of power gifting and dismemberment (death/rebirth) usually happened in quick succession in traditional cultures, but the modern western ego is a tough nut to crack and I've never seen it be so quickly resolved in personal experience. Instead it will usually begin with a 'powering up' process. This can come from power gifts but also the unravelling of Fate-knots that have been previously blocking power. This will feel very good and very exciting, you may even feel like you are high a lot of the time and get quite depressed when these power-highs hit a slough.

It is important to enjoy this time as it's a bit like falling in love, this is where you fall in love with the Craft and as such no other idea should interfere with that enjoyment. In fact, if you are still in this romantic stage of development it might pay you to skip everything else that I've written here and come back to it when you next start to feel a bit confused, frustrated or uncertain about what is going on. Because the harsh truth about the power you gain at this time is that it isn't going to stay with you, at least not in the form it currently takes.

The power injected into you at this stage will function a little like immunization in that it stimulates the immune system to act against it, causing a healing crisis that strengthens the system in the long run. In this case the 'immunization' is the power gifting but the immune system is the ego, the daily self that you are familiar with. Now, because we associated 'ego' with words like egotistical we may think of it as a bad thing. But it most certainly is not. The ego is simply the daily self, and the health of this entity is important.

The ego in fact has its own way of trying to return the self to homeostasis when something is put into it that is judged to be 'Other' or foreign. It reacts in some way against that power. It is this sense of conflict between power that is felt to come from outside the ego and the ego that generates the healing crisis known as being 'made' Initially one might feel it at the onset as a sense of growing conflict between the daily self that has been created over the years of your life and the original self along with all its fetch powers and things they ask of you.

As with anything there is always variety. In some people the ego is comparatively weak. These individuals will suffer less but take longer to reach the point of crisis. Those who possess a very strong ego will need to be hit with a hammer to dislodge it and will find it far more traumatic, but on the good side are likely to make faster progress up to this point, and after it.

For most people the actual crisis will last some months but it could be less or more. It will be a time of confusion and conflict.

The power that has been put in them will be trying to remake that person entirely to recreate them as a more suitable vessel. Of course to the person experiencing this it feels like the threat of death. In fact it is exactly the same thing that happens at death, minus the bodily trauma (usually, though physical sickness is not unheard of).

So it's totally natural that the ego resists it with healthy force. Not only is there the matter of natural fear but also the pressures of daily life that encourage people to stay as they are and not change, so as not to cause anxiety in those around them. Once this begins a process has been set into motion that can only end in two ways. One of them is the death of the ego and the reformation of a self that will be more congenial to future spiritual work. The other is that the person is unable face this and continues in a long drawn out battle that ends with either delusion, ceasing to practice or unconsciously withdrawing from whatever has become associated with the feeling of discomfort.

This is dangerous, high-stakes ground because a half-done making can leave a person very vulnerable and unstable. Assuming that the making comes to a head one should expect at least one, if not a series of, catastrophic visions or dreams. In the vision one may envisage one's helpers taking them apart. You will usually be drawn deeply into the Underworld first, dragged under and even swallowed by something.

Your 'making' might occur as a vision of death and resurrection, or rather than a vision this sensation may go on instead over a couple of days where one is caught in a waking dream. During this time you might wander around quite unable to function, feeling that you are dying or dead. Regardless of how this occurs there will be a final crescendo, a sense of total surrender and self-sacrifice, possibly a rush of universal love and realization of one's littleness in the scheme of the universe's unfolding, a rush of love that conquers fear. The rush of release will be just as intense as the previous spiritual agony. It will feel like a total freedom to be or experience anything you want to, as though total liberation is yours. At this point your fetch and other followers will begin to reconstruct you. They will begin to implant power into you that will stay with you for the rest of your life now, as the building of you as a witch will have truly begun.

The Waters Below the Hills

At the Crossed- Roads gather thyself in solitude and by certain rite perform the Mystery of thine own death.... Here thou shalt learn the pinnacle of the Arte and learn of the death of thy Spirit. Dissolve thy own Quintessence at the centre of the cross and there pass through the moment of all thy deaths - past and future.
-Andrew Chumbley

It is common in many cultures that practice shamanism that there are other smaller trials that the shaman must pass through to gain more power. At the basis of the British mystery traditions, one of the sources that nourish the roots of witchcraft, we have the memory of just one of these practices. In Norse culture it was called the 'mead of inspiration', in Britain it was known as the contents of the 'cauldron of annwn' but basically there is a substance, a kind of liquid fire that is only found deep below the Hollow Hills that when drunk allows access to greater power, wisdom, and memory. We find memories of this substance in folk tales like 'The Forbidden Fountain' were the Fair Folk forbid this one drink to humans who sojourn there, and of course in the 'three drops of Awen' in the story of Taliesin.

For those who find themselves selected to work with the powers of inspiration, creation and wholeness-making through words or music, as represented by the powers of the *Leannan Sidhe* and the path of Awen this is one of the ways one may receive the power of inspiration. The way to get to this source of power, possibly also remembered in the Norse concept of Mimir's Well that Odin loses an eye to get a drink from. This place is so far into the Underworld that only the dead usually venture past that place. To do so may set off another experience of dissolving, a second making. The feelings of being unravelled and challenged in who one is may repeat, though they will be more bearable the second time.

What is faced here more often is a sort of existential crisis, where the true nature of Fate is revealed somewhat and the individual may feel blinded as though they have starred into the face of the Medusa. They question the fundamental 'goodness' of life and even feel a sense of fear just in 'being'. The importance of one's mortal life seems for a time almost unimaginably insignificant. Here people can become waylaid and trapped in the 'whiteness' where they forget to return to the 'redness' of everyday life. In the Thread of witchcraft to which I belong 'whiteness' refers to the Otherworldly side of life; whereas to go on a 'red rest' is to immerse one's self in paying attention to daily, physical life and raising one's vitality.

This stage of intense 'whitening' that we have been discussing will either culminate or be precipitated by a vision of one's fetch-mate luring them deeper in the Underworld than they have ever gone before. You may see yourself swimming down through a lake or well. You will see yourself pass through more layers or doors than you had ever thought possible, usually involving an increasing sense of claustrophobia or pressure as you get deeper and deeper. Eventually you will find yourself very close to the heart of the spiral, the 'eye of the storm' where things are weaved and unweaved. You will need to pass through and to do so you will need to be able to let go of everything of you that is mortal. You will also be stripped of the illusion of 'up' and 'down' and come to realize that in traveling 'down to the bottom' you have also reached the height of heights and are now in the stars.

On the other side there is a substance that can be drunk, it may be in a spring, a cauldron, a chalice or a well, or even sweating from the walls. Drinking it triggers a unitive experience but it also makes you feel you need to flee the place instantly or be unable to return to the Land of the Living. The sense that you are in truth risking never waking up by being there is acutely strong. The true meaning of 'having already died' should become apparent to you in this chamber.

The effect of the fire-waters is inspiration but in saying this it doesn't just mean for creative works. It means for the creation of the self. It is relevant here to think about why what we do is called an 'Art', it takes a certain amount of inspiration to practice any 'art' even if one is not an artist, poet or musician. Drinking the waters seems to trigger the beginning of the incarnation of the original self; its union with the physical body. This part of the work may take years and years. But ultimately you will become an increasingly efficient connection point with the Otherness who's full potential as a many-layered being is beginning to be realized and manifested.

One of the Dead

"A Witch is born out of the true hungers of her time," she said. *"I was born out of New York. The things that are most wrong here summoned me."*
-Ray Bradley

The very nature of the sabbat or the joining of the Furious Horde, by its nature means that the witch joins the company of the dead. Or at least, this can straightforwardly be said to be true with the 'infernal' sabbat and the Wild Hunt (sometimes also called the Furious Horde.) Although not all daimonic entities seem to be souls of dead humans, by virtue of not being 'alive' in the sense that we are, all beings met in the Otherness can in some broader sense be seen as 'the dead', or simply 'the other.' And there is voluminous evidence linking witches with the dead. As Eva Pocs puts it:

Often a group of witches was identified by the most general idea of ghosts, which was the 'communal' dead returning in troops under names like: Shadows... The same kind of dead groups are the 'troops' of witches with flags, a mass of figures in white or black clothes. A troop that arrived at the festival of dead, often at Epiphany, is particularly characteristic: the witches came with their 'evil companions' with eight black and eight red flags on the night of epiphany.[32]

There is evidence also that witches weren't just 'associated with the dead' but actually believed to be among their number and somehow still living among us. We see references to the sent Doubles of witches appearing at the bedside of people wearing white veils or sheets in the manner of ghosts on more than one occasion, but in a Hungarian trial in 1723 this association is made explicit.

In this trial the *late* Mrs Peter Mezei was accused of witchcraft. There was an epidemic of plague and the accusation against her was that she kept returning home and carrying away the people who would then die from plague.[33] This shows us that like a mora-creature a 'witch' or someone to be accused or witchcraft is not necessarily a living human only. Pocs also shows that living witches were sometimes known for have access to the image or second skin of a deceased relative or ancestors, suggesting that witches (like shamans in some other cultures) were considered to be literally 'the dead returned' in that they were the reincarnation of elder witches.

All of this might simply sound strange, the idea of a living, breathing person being seen as 'one of the dead' if we hadn't already discussed initiation. Initiation in most shamanic cultures is about death and dying. The person that was a not a witch, shaman or sorcerer is killed or dismembered and a new person is resurrected to do their work in the land of the living, but that person is no longer who they were before. They occupy the same space but they now manifest uncanny energies and powers. For this reason they may achieve change and even healing, but they may also be a focal point for anxiety or fear. Like all of the dead that the witch is in fact one with, the witch may bring either guardianship or harm to his or her community, depending on how they have been treated by them.

Ritual Space

Due to the influence of ceremonial magic we tend to find most modern witches very concerned about how they set up 'ritual space.' There is a strong focus on creating barriers of protection or spaces between the worlds. There is not a lot of evidence to suggest that witches worked in 'circles'. We have some evidence of talismanic forms of protection such as the five pointed star being used in Wales and elsewhere to protect an area or on a child's cradle. Methods of protection appear to have been numerous in past folklore. Objects like witches boots and witch-bottles were installed in walls, in chimneys and buried around the property, as a method of diversionary magic, that is to mimic the personal power of the person they were meant to protect and attract evil to a decoy.

Of course there were also other more expected forms of protection such as iron talismans against faerie intrusion, garlic against vampiric entities and various remedies like rowan, trefoil and dill to repel 'witches.' Just as faerie magic is interfered with by iron, it was also understood in the past that witches can't 'spell' past objects of brass; which may be the original meaning of the geometric shapes that form most of the traditional 'horse brasses' of the British Isles.

Many if not all of this battery of protective charms should probably be utilised by the modern witch to keep a spiritually safe home and working area. Especially if one intends to bring the forces outside the hedge inside the hedge, these protective charms will then become very important. There is, however, no entirely folkloric method of 'barrier magic' that is designed to wrap a circle about the practitioners.

The idea of associating witches with circles probably originally arose from the fairy ring phenomenon, a circle of mushrooms or other fungi believed to be made by dancing faeries, that were sometimes called *hexenringe* or 'witches rings.' These of course are an organic shape meant to reflect a circular dance, rather than a ceremonial object drawn to keep out demons.

The other purpose often ascribed to modern revivialist 'circle casting' is that it creates 'sacred space.' The faerie-doctor seems to have drawn a ring about themselves with charcoal from a stick with a burned tip (see below the entry on 'Faerie-Doctoring') in the dirt or on the floor when about to conduct a healing or divination. Despite this example, for most witches of the past it appears that this function of sanctifying a space was mainly fullfilled by simply calling to their spirit or familiar spirits, or offering some food or blood to them.

In our coven both the protection and the 'sanctifying of space' is carried out via the agency of the familiar spirits and every ritual begins with a stirring up of the spirits and involves them being offered smoke and roused by drumming (as with the faerie drummer) or by rattles or bells or whistling for them, or by any other method that the witch has been instructed to call to the spirit. There is plenty of traditional material to suggest the offering of smoke to spirits, such as the burning of dragons blood on the fire in Welsh folklore[34] before a divination and John Walsh, a witch of the West Country who burned frankincense and St Johns wort before his operations. Of course the grimoires of Ceremonial Magic also furnish us forth with complex sumfumigations that can be burned to aid spirit manifestation.

If concerns about magical security remain after a ritual has been performed in a family home one may protect themselves and their family by sprinkling salt over the working area, and sweeping it out the door with a broom. One should then inscribe a peice of wood or leather with a pentacle and the words:

Rotas, Opera, Arepo, Sator

And thus have the object wrapped up and hidden somewhere close to the place where witchcraft is generally performed in the home.[35]

This all being said, there are certain operations for which a full witches ring should be cast, particularly for works of necromancy and exorcism. Traditional Witchcraft in the modern era tends to make use of both a circle and a 'Triangle of Art.' The witch stands within the circle, and the triangle is usually placed outside the circle in either the east or the north, depending on the type of working (east for exorcism, north for necromancy), with the tip of the triangle facing away from the circle.

Whilst this practice has clearly been absorbed from grimoires at some point, it has become so thoroughly absorbed into Traditional Craft that some comment upon it is necessary. The following explanation for the circle and the triangle in Traditional Witchcraft was given to me specifically in relation to necromancy, so that must be kept in mind.

The circle is cast widdershins to represent the descent into the Underworld. Although only the outer circle is delineated you should be aware that the circle is not in fact a circle but a spiral, a downward leading staircase. After you depict the circle in this world, with chalk or cord and call in your familiars to empower it, begin to slowly and meditatively walk widdershins in an ever decreasing spiral until your each the centre. Do so with your eyes slightly closed so that you are 'turning inward' as you physically turn inward. In this way the circle/spiral becomes your own depths and the Underworld's depths and makes those two places one. In other words it takes you down to the depths and brings the depths up to you. So the spiral exists in you as well as in the circle which is also the Underworld, it exists in the back of your skull.

When you have done this you will turn to the Triangle of Art. The Triangle of Art represents the 'gift of fire', it is the spark of fire that allows Art, just as the circle is the Underworld and your deep mind. In witchcraft the circle is not so much a barrier but a cauldron that seethes. You draw up from the spiralling darkness the spirit you wish to have in the triangle. The triangle is your divine spark, located at the front of your brain, the jewel upon your forehead that the Master gifted you with.

Once inside the triangle of fire the spirit has been drawn up from the realms of unconsciousness into the realms of consciousness, in other words you have become aware of them. The magic that allows you to call them there is indeed the magic of the spark of divine fire, symbolised by the triangle, but to draw the dead there in the first place you must be capable of sinking into the darkness and drawing it up through your own being. There are no utter barriers between witches and anything else, all fire and all shadow comes through us, we are only conduits.

Discovering the Fetch-Beast

For those who don't already dream of or as an animal they may a yet have some intuition about what creature will come to them; they may have had a fascination with a particular type of animal all their life. But this is not always the case, it is not enough for you to like that animal in the manner so often used with neo-pagan 'totem animals', this spirit must choose you. Your own intuition can however help you to construct a list of possibilities. Begin with common fetch-creatures of Europe: Fox, Mouse, Dog, Weasel, Toad, Wolf, Hawk, Cat, Bat, Badger, Eagle, Raven, Snake, Horse, Bear, Deer, Owl and Boar. You will notice that predatory animals tend to out number prey animals. Only creatures of extreme physical power like wild horses and stags are the exception to this rule usually. Or small animals like mice that have strengths involving secrecy, cunning and adaptability.

For this divination[36] you will need a knife or dagger that will be wrapped in a 'winding sheet' of white material at least a few feet long and only so wide as it covers the entire knife when wrapped. Wrap the knife around in the white material until none of it is visible. For three nights previously leave offerings of milk for the animal asking it to reveal itself to you on the third night. It is good to remember, when dealing with the faeries in general, that milk is appropriate for animal spirits unless something more specific is asked of you. Leave these offerings over night and pour them out on a stone outside you keep for this purpose in the morning. Leave these offerings next to the hearth or near your back door mat outside.

On the final night after placing your offering go to a hedge or fence, somewhere that marks the boundary of your property. You need to put one foot partially through the fence so that you are 'riding the hedge.' When this is done say: "Fetch-beast reveal your nature to me." Then begin to pass the covered knife from hand to hand counter-clockwise about your body. On the first circle say: "My fetch-beast is a mouse," on the second: "My fetch-beast is a fox." This should be done in no particular order but as the names of the animals occur to you. The animal will reveal itself by disarranging the white winding-sheet and allowing the dagger to show. Take note of what animal you had just named before the dagger was exposed.

Bow or curtsy to the spirit and leave the place. Note the animal down but do not do anything or offer anything at this point. Sometimes soon after beginning to enquire in this manner something will happen to spontaneously confirm what you have been told, or to tell you something else entirely different. Here is a testimonial from a modern witch who had done this divination and was still uncertain what her fetch-beast might be:

I had a dream about a week later that a red dog came out of a hedge and turned into a black dog, the black dog came up and was really comforting and warm, then he turned into two cats sitting on top of me and purring, purring, purring. Again I didn't catch on, because well, there were cats and dogs in the dream. And at the time I wasn't aware that the black dog was the familiar of another witch who I knew a little.

However about a week after that I was dozing, not asleep. I was awake enough to hear the children, but asleep enough to be receptive. I felt a cat jump up onto the bed and walk on top of me smooching up to me and purring, purring, purring. I snapped my eyes open to check if it was one of our cats. I knew it wasn't, partly since the bedroom door was shut and partly it was smaller and softer than ours, but since it felt exactly like a real cat I opened my eyes. Nope. Nothing. I closed them again and almost immediately felt the cat jump onto the bed again, and come sweetly up to rub around my face. Eventually she settled on top of me, just like the cats in the dream, and purred so that it made my whole body vibrate. She was there a long time and it felt exactly as if it was real. A little later I realised I was wide-awake and she was gone.

-Modern witch

Doning the Mask

After burning incense appropriate to your daimonic self go into a light meditative state. Visualise before you a mask, give it all the properties that you would consider to be most opposite to your daily nature. It must be antithetical to yourself, that is, where you are sensitive it must be brash and bold, it should probably be given Marsian and Jupiterian qualities, or where you are bold and brash the mask should instead be lunar and watery in quality. Mentally construct this mask that gets across all these things you find to be most outside of yourself. Gaze at the image until you have a very clear sense of it pulsing out that power at you. Then when you feel it almost able to stare back at you, visualize yourself reaching out and placing the mask on.

What happens here is that by merging with everything that you reject and find least comfortable a Third thing emerges which is neither, the original self which you will find has a talent for resolving contradictions inside it's own completeness. When you feel that Third thing that is neither the daily self, nor the anti-self-mask merge you will be in the perfect state to attract the fetch-mate. You may proceed to interact with the fetch-mate or simply sit and be in this state. Either way, the fetch-mate will be attracted by you in your Wholeness.[37]

Acquiring a Magical Assistant

The following rite, adapted by me from the Greek Magical Papyri is designed to attract a daimon to those who are without one or who have not reason to believe that they have been thus visited. To prepare for the rite one must abstain from animal food for a week and also abstain from sex or masturbation for three nights to retain ones vital forces. Go to an outdoors location, preferably a high place in a pure garment just washed, right before the dawn. Intone:

'IAEOBAPHRENEMOUN' and the formula **'IARBATHA.'**

Say this as you burn frankincense and pure rose oil in an earthen censer on ashes from the plant heliotrope, if this plant can be found. While you burn this go into a light meditative trance. You must then await a sign. The traditional sign was that something would be seen to descend from the sky and leave a token for you. If some form of omen that seems significant enough occurs, possibly in the form of a bird or other creature then you should proceed.

That evening you this time face the moon and burn myrrh in the same manner that you burned the frankincense. Use a myrtle bough to cense the area and offer this smoke to The Lady, who is patron of such pairings between mortals and immortals. There should be another sign, you may feel you see this 'in your mind's eye' but it may appear as a shooting star or other flash of light. At this point the operation will only succeed if the witch is able to perceive spirits or obtain a light trance. For it is now that the daimon will appear if one has decided to grant its presence to you. It is said that you should approach the daimon and take his right hand and kiss him. When you have done so it was traditional to say:

I abjure you with this oath that you remain inseparable and not be silent with me.

I would have you as friend, assistant and come together for loving benefit, who harms not and answers when I say 'appear on earth to me'.

When the daimon agrees to this it is said that you take his hand and 'jump down' into your working space. I take this to mean that you have been either entirely outside or partially outside your body during this operation and that you now offer to draw the daimon down temporarily into your world of the flesh. The lure for joining you here involves a well-set feast that you have laid out in offering including fine wine and possibly some 'reclining' together. It is said that he may stay for no more than three hours and that before you let him go and whenever you wish to call him back you should call him back with the words:

Come to me, King/Queen, [I call you] my god of gods, mighty one, boundless and undefiled one, indescribable and of great age. Be inseparable from me from this day forth through all the time of my life and lives.

Faerie-Doctoring

The following operation is for the use of those witches who find themselves gifted with the attentions of faerie and possessing a healing gift. For the purposes of this rite the operant will be called the 'faerie-doctor.'[38] The healing is meant to be done for another person who is suffering from an inexplicable illness that may be the result of faerie malevolence.

The faerie-doctor takes three rods of witch hazel, each three inches long, and marks them separately, 'For the Stroke,' (this refers to someone slowly pining away for faerie related reasons, usually because someone in faerie wants them for a partner) 'For the Wind,' (an ill wind sent my faeries that one was meant to avoid being outside in that displays a kind of random seeming general faerie malevolence) 'For the Evil Eye.' (those who were overlooked or cursed by a human witch, showing the faerie-doctor's role as curse breaker.) This is to ascertain from which of these three preternatural evils the patient suffers.

The faerie-doctor must take off his or her coat, shoes, and stockings; roll up his shirtsleeves, and stand with his face to the sun in earnest prayer. After prayer he will take a dish of pure water and sets it by the fire, then kneeling down, he must put the three hazel rods he has marked into the fire, and leave them there till they are burned black. All the time the prayers are unceasing; and when the sticks are burned, he rises, and again faces the sun in silent prayer, standing with his eyes uplifted and hands crossed. After this he will draw a circle on the floor with the end of one of the burned sticks, within which circle he stands, the dish of pure water beside him. Into this he will fling the three hazel rods, and watches the result earnestly.

The moment one sinks he addresses a prayer to the sun, and taking the rod out of the water he declares by what agency the patient is afflicted. Then he will grind the rod to powder, puts it in a bottle that he fills up with water from the dish, and utters an incantation or prayer over it, in a low voice, with clasped hands held over the bottle. The potion is then given to the patient to be carried home, and drunk that night at midnight in silence and alone. Great care must be taken that the bottle never touches the ground. This rule that the medicine must not touch the ground is a hallmark of faerie healing magic. There is a fire in the medicine, much like the sun that is prayed to in this ritual that is 'grounded' if the herb or medicine touches the earth.

The person carrying it must also speak no word, and never look back behind them till they reach home. The other two sticks he buries in the earth in some place unseen and unknown. If none of the three sticks sink in the water, then he uses herbs as a cure. Vervain, Eyebright, and Yarrow are favourite herbs of the faerie - doctor, and it can be imagined that he or she knew the special songs and prayers by which to speak with this small number of plant-helpers they primarily worked with. If a potion is made up of herbs it must be paid for in 'silver'; but charms and incantations are never paid for, or they would lose their power. A present, however, may be accepted as an offering of gratitude.

Skin-Faring

It is helpful to keep in mind that when I talk about a 'second skin' I am using this term advisedly instead of 'subtle body' or 'etheric Double' because it's important that we remember its semi-corporeal nature. Fully activating it and getting it to leave the body is not the same as being in your 'daimonic self', the daimonic or 'original self', instead is what inhabits the Skins. Most sorcerers have multiple different Skins this is why we are called skin-turners. Most of us possess one that is a Double of our daily human form, and another in an animal form, and some have even more than this or have a talent for merging more than one. Creatures that have a dizzying array of transformations available are usually using glamours or 'hag riding' the Skins of other creatures.

When you would begin to awaken the ability to turn your skin, sink down slightly so that your awareness tingles around the part of your body touching the bed. It is best for this exercise to by lying down. Feel for the tingling of power in your body. Pay attention to the tingling and try to delineate its shape. Focus on this sensation until you feel as though you could tug something slightly out of your flesh. This should be a very visceral sensation, try tugging and pulling and rocking the second skin back and forth within your daily body. Try to rock or sway or even tremble it whilst keeping your daily body still. When you have a sense of its corporeal, almost sticky quality, begin to slightly pull it free. This should give you a shimmering sensation in the head. But do not separate the bodies, simply ask your daimonic self to invigorate this second skin, recognise it, fill it with fire.

After a few weeks of practicing this technique in tandem with the *Donning the Mask* technique try to combine them. Use 'Donning the Mask' to *become* your daimonic self and then while you are in that state begin this exercise. Eventually you will find yourself able to introduce the daimonic self into the second skin and go into flight in this heightened manner. It is in this way that the most intense encounters with the fetch-mate can then occur, and the full function that one is to perform in the Otherworld is best learned. Of course combining these practices with the advice I have given earlier in the book in regards to sleep patterns and 'twilight time' will also greatly enhance your success.

Calling to the Devil

The so-called 'Devil' is greatly important to witchcraft, but primarily in the form of the Magistellus, or 'little master' that attends a coven as the 'devil of the coven'. Originally this tradition may have begun in something similarly to the legend of the The Watchers that we discussed in the chapter on fetch-mates. The devil of the coven having carnal intercourse with all of the witches may have occured because that Magistellus had personally taken on those witches to tutor and inspire them and fill them each with his fire.

This aspect of the relationship with the Magistellus may not be quite the same in covens where each is attended by a daimonic intelligence with whom they have a sacred marriage pact. Isobel Gowdies' coven, however, did seem to keep up a tradition of each of the witches having personal spirits seemingly of the opposite sex themselves, as well as relations with the coven devil.

The following chant is a traditional one from Welsh folkloric sources and may be repeated or used in a round while smoke is burned to call the Magistellus to be present with his witches. Of course the final line is omitted until such time as the Maid/Magistra or Magister of the coven intuits it's time to bring the chant to a close:

> One two, three and four
> The devil is at the door.
> Make him welcome from floor to roof,
> Drink to him in a horse's hoof.
> Bring the cat and the toad and the bran,
> Come to the feast as ye who can.
> One, two, three and four,
> The devil is here, so no more!

Exorcism

When we think of 'exorcism' we tend to think of Christian rites for driving out the Devil and his demons. Here I aim to provide a workable practice for removing troublesome influences from a person or a dwelling within a non-Christian framework, using a combination of traditional formulae.

The first thing that is required for one to undertake a successful exorcism is a talent in this area, I cannot stress this enough. Necromancers are a particular type of witch, though any witch might make forays into necromancy, not all will be equally gifted in it, the same goes for healing and exorcism. Exorcism is a kind of spiritual combat and therefore tends to belong to witches of the *benandanti* and *táltos* type, the ecstatic sorcerers who battled for their community. For this reason excorcisms are best practice on a Thursday.

The second thing that needs to be acknowledged is that we have to remove the weight of Christian baggage. Movies and books about Christian exorcisms tend to present an implacable and terrifying enemy of great and mysterious power. The Devil and demons are a mystery to Christians, part of a dark netherworld that they have no access to. The witches' interaction with spirits is different.

Spirits of death, darkness and disease are not a complete unknown to us. All powers, no matter how dangerous, have a sacred and appropriate place in creation, this includes ones we do battle with and things we kill and injure in self defence. Just as the Siberian shaman was initiated by the 'smallpox spirit' and devoured by evil spirits and in return gained some power and understanding of their world, the witch gains power over the realms of darkness by being part of that darkness. Do not allow yourself to be intimidated by a haunting or a possession, if you are intimidated you are already half beaten. These spirits may be negotiated with and you may be able to make them leave by offering them things in return for doing so. Do not ever undertake to 'clear' a location forcefully if you are able to do it via negotiation.

Disturbances requiring exorcism may be either centered on a person or a location. By and large the procedure is the same for both in that you must begin by making contact with the entity or entities and finding out why they are there and what they want. A penduluum may come in handy here so that the person with the affliction may see the answers being given and feel part of the process. No witch who doubts their ability to communicate with spirits ought to be undertaking an exorcism. In a case where the spirit cannot be convinced to depart with offerings then the following formula can be used to force the removal of the entity.

Have the person to be exorcised stand on a cross of salt drawn on the floor. (If the exorcism is on a location place one of these equal armed crosses in each corner of the house). The witch is to have prepared a bundle of fern, pine and rue into a sort of switch that is large enough to sweep over the person's body from the head down towards the feet whilst they are speaking (or the extremities of the property where appropriate). The witch should also be standing so as to be touching the salt with their foot or have salt in their shoes if moving around. Whilst this is performed the witch says:

By the power of the Master, and of the Lady, and of my Familiar Spirit X, let this disease depart, and the spell of the evil spirits be broken! I adjure, I command you to depart from this man or woman [naming him or her] out of his bones, his blood, his veins, his joints. In the name of Grandmother Weaver I pray; in the name of the holy fire I abjure; in the name of the divine fire within I command and compel you to go back and leave this man free! It shall be done! It shall be done! It shall be done!

The last part is said with some passion.

This is repeated over and over again whilst a great fiery power of wrath is generated in the exorcist's body. It is this ability of self-excitation in conjunction with the power of their familiar spirits that will determine the outcome of the exorcism.

There will be a feeling of sudden weightlessness that might even make the exorcist feel dizzy when the spirit relinquishes its hold. At this point the words cease and a hand-rolled tobacco cigarette or pipe must be produced. The witch then produces a bottle that is corkable and has some alcoholic spirits inside it. The witch blows the tobacco smoke down into the bottle whilst holding out the bottle near the body of the person being exorcized.

The smoke encourages the spirit to enter the bottle that is then corked and thrown into the ocean or buried. The spirit will of course get free of this bottle and afflict something else, so exorcism is a form of transferal of ills to a place where they are unlikely to return and afflict the patient. To slow down the spirit's ability to get free the bottle can be filled with hundreds of grains of sand or multiple threads with hundreds of knots. The entity will then be forced to count each grain or knot before it will be able to get free.

It should perhaps go without saying that nobody should go into an exorcism situation who is not feeling 'powered up' and vigorous and that the exorcist should first call their protective spirits and have upon them numerous talismans and protective items.[39]

Making Healing Water

This tradition of making healing water with the use of a spherical crystal is attested to both in Wales and Ireland. As it is an example of a healing spell it belongs quite closely to the tradition of faerie-doctoring and curse breaking within a softer current of power than that of exorcism and spirit battle. The crystal ball was held in a basin of water and the following charm was said:

> *O thou stone of Night and Right*
> *Let me dip thee in water.*
> *In the water of the pure spring or of wave,*
> *In the name of Our Lady*
> *And the Mothers of my line,*
> *In the name of the Master of Magic*
> *And all the Master-men.*
> *Blessings on the clear pure water!*
> *A healing of all bodily ills*
> *On man and beast alike!*

The water was then able to heal and drive out evil afflictions. But if someone came to use someone else's crystal ball or must take home the healing water afterwards then certain rules apply. The person coming to fetch the ball or fetching the water home again must not speak, sit, or enter the person's home and on the way home they must not remain out of doors after sunset. These prohibits tell us a lot about the operation. Just as in the faerie-doctoring the sun is important, for the crystal must not be out of doors after the sun is gone. The prohibition on speaking is also the same as when taking home the faerie- doctor's cure. Water made after this traditional formulae could also be utilised to cleanse areas of malignant influence.[40]

A Rite of Necromancy

The art of necromancy as it is commonly presented in grimoires suffers from the same weaknesses as exorcism, being that it is full of Christian material that may not work ideologically for a witch. Secret names for the god Jehovah do not fit terribly well within the cosmological framework we have developed here, so in this necromantic working I have attempted to bring the best of the 'grimoire tradition' into a witchcraft context.

The first and very important step is to prepare yourself adequately. Some witches are natural necromancers who have a developed relationship with the dead and death powers just by nature. Such necromantic witches may not require too much preparation to contact the world of the dead, but it is nonetheless helpful to know how.

The witch must align their mind with the unseen by meditating and refraining from drinking or consuming anything warm for that day. Doing the operation in a location such as a cemetary or crossroads is also another time honoured practice, but failing this one must gather together objects that carry this power, such as bones, ashes, grave dirt, or body parts of people or animals.

The witch will also require something sharp for the purposes of letting blood and a sermon timer-style hour glass, preferrably one that is set to run for about twenty minutes. A Triangle of Art is also needed, but this may simply be drawn on the ground in chalk if necessary. Some black candles, incense and any relics of the deceased will also be needed. The witch will draw a circle on the floor and the triangle will be placed in the northern quarter with its point facing away from the circle. In the spirit of strict minimalism this operation is possible with: chalk, hour glass, scalpel, candles, incense and charcoal, and some kind of magical weapon (wand, staff, dagger.)

1. Place two black candles in the northern quarter inside the circle with some matches and your prepared incense (recipe below).

2. Place your censor inside the triangle with charcoal prepared for incense, along with any relics of the deceased and a picture if possible.

3. Surround the circle with items of death of they are available.

4. Light the candle and the incense charcoal.

5. Call your familiar spirits to aid you and strengthen your circle and hold that space.

6. Call upon a force that presides over the dead. The original rite calls upon Hecate with a poetic incantation, followed by an ad-lib request for the deity's help in successfully completing the operation. It will help immensely if the Underworldian deity you call to is one you offer to at least semi regularly.

7. Place fresh incense on the charcoal.

8. Blow out the candles and call upon the spirit of the deceased. As you do so try to feel the ground dropping away under you, as though the very ground beneath you were suddenly an abyss and you yourself were sinking partially into the Underworld to draw this shade back up with you. This is the symbolism behind the blowing out and the relighting of the candles. Only say the words when you can already feel the brooding presence of the deceased in the shadows that churn beneath you and are already reaching out your hand to draw them up with you.

Colpriziana, offina alta nestra, fuaro menut, i name .... the dead which i seek, ... thou art the dead that i seek. Spirit of ......, deceased, you may now approach this gate and answer truly to my calling. Berald, Beroald, Balbin, Gab, Gabor, Agaba! Arise, I charge and call thee.

9. Make an X sign with your sorcerous weapon, calling the person's name. When there is a feeling or sight of a manifestation in the smoke, Say to it: "**Allay Fortission Fortissio Allynsen Roa!**" –Which seems to say to the deceased that your offer them breath and fortitude. This refers to your willingness to supply some of your own life force to the shade for its manifestation, hence the hourglass that times this interaction!

10. Turn over the hourglass and when and if you feel ready relight the candles so as to better see or make notes. The symbolism of this is drawing the dead up into the light of the world above.

11. Do your business with the deceased for as long as the sand in the hour glass runs.

12. When the sand runs out say **"Go, Go departed shades by Omgroma Epic Sayoc, Satony, Degony, Eparigon, Galiganon, Zogogen, Ferstigon. I License thee to depart unto thy proper place and be there peace between us evermore."**

The incense should be composed of oil, red wine, wormwood, gum mastic, storax, pinch of the deceased's grave dirt and the operator's blood. The blood and its freshness are important so open the wound and bleed into the incense at the last moment before opening the ritual. In this way necromancers, especially those who have a talent for such things, achieve very strong manifestations and communications. However one should be careful to realign with 'life' powers after such operations through eating and drinking and warming oneself and perhaps sexual intercourse. [41]

Conclusion

We regard witchcraft as part of the mystery of our cultural heritage.
    -Steve Bico

To access what some people call the 'tradition' of witchcraft we need to first understand that witchcraft as we know it today is a myth. But this is not to say it doesn't exist. The 'nameless deed' that lies behind that myth is part of the eternal nature of mankind. But it is also universally part of human nature to experience the divine and the transcendent through the conduit of myth.

The divine seems to like to dress in myth, story, narrative – but most especially myth, that thing that happens when story is raised to its highest possible potential. Myth behaves as a kind of foyer or meeting place where gods, spirits and man can meet and make sense of each other. The 'myth of witchcraft', where numerous and diverse spiritual motifs and experiences became unified under this one usually reviled word, is one such meeting place.

At first it may seem to be a broken myth, full of fragments and distortion, but if we apply the light of up to date scholarship, hand in hand with the darkness of our own occult intuition and experience as passed down from initiated witch to initiated witch, I believe that this is not in fact the case.

Far from being broken, the myth of witchcraft, something which feeds the roots of the practices today known as Traditional Witchcraft, still shelters the essence of the fundamental 'deed without a name' and allows us access to it, if we truly belong to its story. This book stands as a genuine attempt to gather together the threads of light and dark and of the half light, as Yeats would put it, and to contribute to the salvaging of this crucial component of the spiritual heritage of Europe.

Appendix

Planetary Correspondences

The following is a very basic run-down on planetary correspondences as they relate to the witchcraft presented in this book. For Cornelius Agrippa's classic source material on this subject please see the following site:

http://altreligion.about.com/od/planetarycorrespondences/Planetary_Correspondences.htm

Or for a table that has been adapted to suit Traditional Witchcraft and includes herbs and colours, please see Robin Artisson's *The Horn of Evenwood: A Grimoire of Sorcerous Operations, Charms and Devices of Witchery.*

As you will see many phenomena cross over into more than one category and we seldom find a complex spirit that can be easily described by a single planetary current.

Lunar

Day of the Week: Monday

Witchcraft Matters: Psychism, Dreams, Second Sight, Female Fertility, Illusion, Intuition, Divination.

Associated Beings: Mermaids, Selkies, Werewolves, *Donas de fuera*, Water-horse.

Marsian

Day of the Week: Tuesday

Witchcraft Matters: Vengeance, Male Virility, 'Hot' cursing,

Violent weather, Spirit Combat.

Associated Beings: *Benandanti, Táltos,* Werewolves,

Mercurial
Day of the Week: Wednesday

Witchcraft Matters: Trance, Inspiration, Intellect, Trickery, Cunning, Imagination, Transformation, Shape-Changing.

Associated Beings: Faeries and Faerie-Magicians, Awenyddion, Liderc, Fox-People.

Jupiterian
Day of the Week: Thursday

Witchcraft Matters: Defence, Protection, Sacrifice, Leadership, Protection of home, Exorcism.

Associated Beings: *Benandanti,* Cunning Men and Curse-Breakers of all kinds, Snake-Men, Protective Spirits of the Home.

Venusian
Day of the Week: Friday

Witchcraft Matters: Seduction, Lust, Love Spells, Fertility, Beauty, Pleasure, Natural Magic.

Associated Beings: Succubae, Nymphs, Practitioners of Erotic Sorcery, *Leannan Sidhe,* The Fetch-Mate in general, *Ganconagh.*

Saturnian
Day of the Week: Saturday

Witchcraft Matters: Death, Initiation, Binding, 'Black' curses, Fate-weaving, Necromancy.

Associated Beings: Beansidhe, Mazzeri, Hell-Hounds, Vampiric entities, Mora/Mara Creatures, The Dead, Ancestral Fate-figures.

Solar

Day of the Week: Sunday

Witchcraft Matters: Healing, Insight, Exorcism, Diagnostic Workings, Purification, Rejuvenation, Joy.

Associated Beings: The Shining Court, Faerie-Doctors, Snake-men, Exorcists, Spirits of the Hearth Fire.

References

1. Carlos Ginzburg, *The Night Battles: Witchcraft and Agrarian Cults in the Sixteenth and Seventeenth Centuries.*, John Hopkins Press, (1993)

2. Eva Pocs, *Between the Living and the Dead.*, Central European University Press, Budapest. (1999)

3. Claude Lecouteux, *The Return of the Dead: Ghosts, Ancestors and the Transparent Veil of the Pagan Mind.*, Inner Traditions, (2009)

4. Emma Wilby, *The Visions of Isobel Gowdie: Magic, Witchcraft and Dark Shamanism in Seventeenth-Century Scotland.*, Sussex Academic Press, (2011)

5. Laszlo Kurti, The Way of the Taltos: A Critical Reassessment of a Religious Magical Specialist, Mythologica Slavica., Edition Three, (2000) p.93

6. Nigel Pennick, *The Celtic Saints: An Illustrated and Authoritative Guide to these Extraordinary Men and Women.*, Godsfield Press., (1997) p.98

7. All terminology is explained in detail in the section marked: Bestiary.

8. Laszlo Kurti, The Way of the Taltos: A critical reassessment of a Religious-Magical specialist., *Studia Mythologica Slavica, Edition Three*, 2000, 89, 114

9. Eva Pocs, *op cit.*, p.38

10. Hubert J Davis, *The Silver Bullet: and other American witch stories.*, Johnathon David Publishers. (1975) p.80

11. Emma Wilby, *op cit.*, p.250

12. Robert Kirk, Andrew Lang, *The Secret Commonwealth of Elves, Fauns and Fairies.*, Aberyfoyle, Scotland. Forgotten Books. (2010) p. 39

13. W.B Yeats, *Fairy and Folk Tales of the Irish Peasantry.* (1888)

14. Carlos Ginzburg, *The Night Battles.*, p.35

15. Eva Pocs, *op cit.*, p.32
16. Eva Pocs, op cit., p. 130
17. Carlos Ginzburg, *The Night Battles.*, p.33
18. Emma Wilby, *op cit.*, pp. 498-499
19. Graham Hancock's book *Supernatural* though written as an adventure story as much as a work of scholarship, gathers together a vast array of primary source material on this topic.
20. Margaret Murray, *God of the Witches.*, Oxford University Press, (1970) p.23
21. http://www.underworldtales.com/basque.htm
22. Adapted from text provided by Emma Wilby, *op cit.*, p.47
23. John Michael Greet, *The New Encyclopaedia of the Occult.*, Llwellyn Worldwide., (2004) p.353
24. Robert Kirk, *op cit.*, p.57
25. Ploss, H.: Das Kind in Brauch und Sitte der Völker. Leipzig, Grieben, 1884, 1, p. 298.
26. Hofler, M.: Deutsches Krankheitsnwmen-Buch. Munchen, Piloty & Loehle, 1899, p. 414.
27. The Examination and Confession of Certain Witches at Chelmsford in the County of Essex, before the Queen Majesty's Judges, the 26th day of July Anno 1566 (London, 1566)
28. Eva Pocs, *op cit.*, p.47
29. Eva Pocs, *op cit.*, p.88
30. Lady Wilde, *Fairy and Folk Tales of the Irish Peasantry.*, http://www.sacred-texts.com/neu/yeats/fip/fip43.htm (2012)
31. W.Y Evans-Wentz, *The Faerie Faith in Celtic Countries,* Forgotten Books, (2007) p. 120
32. Pocs, *op cit.*, p.41
33. Pocs, *op cit.*, p.42
34. Marie Trevelyan, Folklore and Folk Stories of Wales., P Publishing Ltd; Facsimile of 1909 ed edition (1973) p.154
35. The protective charm used here is sourced from: Marie

Trevelyan, *op cit.*, p.151

36. Ristandi, *The Hidden Link Between Lik and Fylgia.*, *Rune-Kevels* Vol. IX no. 2 [NS# 36] The Rune Gild, 2001
37. This meditation is adapted from a practice used by W.B Yeats
38. This healing ritual is adapted from information given by Lady Wilde in her *Ancient Legends, Mystic Charms, and Superstitions of Ireland,* (1887)
39. The words in this exhortation are put together from combined sources one being from an Irish faerie-doctor another from a Welsh conjurer. The use of the alcohol and tobacco is mildly influenced by Hoodoo.
40. Marie Trevelyan, p. 150
41. This ritual is inspired in part by the *Grimorium Verum* as well as by the Fourth Book of Agrippa.

Further Reading

Agrippa, Cornelius, *Three Books of Occult Philosophy*

Alibeck the Egyptian, *Grimorium Verum*

Apuleius, The Golden Ass

Artisson, Robin, *The Witching Way of the Hollow Hill*

Artisson, Robin, *The Horn of Evenwood: A Grimoire of Sorcerous Operations, Charms and Devices of Witchery.*

Cochrane, Robert, *The Robert Cochrane Letters: An Insight Into Modern Traditional Witchcraft*

Chumbley, Andrew, *Azoetia: A Grimoire of the Sabbatic Craft*

Chumbley, Andrew, *One: The Grimoire of the Golden Toad*

Davis, Hubert J. *The Silver Bullet and other American Witch Stories*

Eliade, Mircea, *Shamanism*

Evans-Wentz, W.Y, *The Faerie Faith in Celtic Countries*

Glanvill, Joseph, *Saducismus triumphatus*

Ginzburg, Carlos, *Ecstasies: Deciphering the Witches Sabbath*

Ginzburg, Carlos, *The Night Battles: Witchcraft and Agrarian Cults in the Sixteenth and Seventeenth Centuries*

Grammary, Ann, *The Witch's Workbook*

Greek Magical Papyri

Hancock, Graham, *Supernatural*

Harner, Michael, *The Way of the Shaman*

Huson, Paul, *Mastering Witchcraft*

Jackson, Nigel, *Call of the Horned Piper*

Jackson, Nigel and Howard, Michael, *The Pillars of Tubal Cain*

Kirk, Robert, and Lang, Andrew, *The Secret Commonwealth of Elves, Fauns and Fairies*

Lecouteux, Claude, *The Return of the Dead: Ghosts, Ancestors and the Transparent Veil of the Pagan Mind*

Lecouteux, Claude, *Witches, Werewolves and Fairies*

Scot, Reginald, *The Discoverie of Witchcraft*

Trevelyan, Marie, *Folklore and Folk Stories of Wales*

Pocs, Eva, *Between the Living and the Dead*

Wilby, Emma, *The Visions of Isobel Gowdie: Magic, Witchcraft and Dark Shamanism in Seventeenth-Century Scotland*

Wilde, Lady Jane, *Fairy and Folk Tales of the Irish Peasantry*

Yeats, Y.B, *The Celtic Twilight*

MOON
BOOKS

Moon Books invites you to begin or deepen your encounter with Paganism, in all its rich, creative, flourishing forms.